22,95

S0-ARM-611

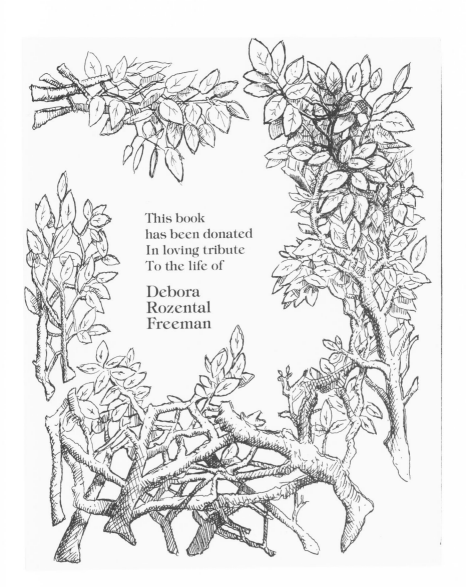

This book
has been donated
In loving tribute
To the life of

**Debora
Rozental
Freeman**

Willa Cather

Revised Edition

Twayne's United States Authors Series

Joseph M. Flora, General Editor

University of North Carolina, Chapel Hill

TUSAS 258

WILLA CATHER BY EDWARD STEICHEN
Reprinted with permission of Joanna T. Steichen

Willa Cather

Revised Edition

Philip Gerber

State University of New York, Brockport

Twayne Publishers
An Imprint of Simon & Schuster Macmillan
New York

Prentice Hall International
London • Mexico City • New Delhi • Singapore • Sydney • Toronto

HIGHLAND PARK PUBLIC LIBRARY
494 Laurel Avenue
Highland Park, IL 60035

813
C36
Zg. 2

Twayne's United States Authors Series No. 258

Willa Cather, Revised Edition
Philip Gerber

Copyright © 1995 by Twayne Publishers
All rights reserved. No part of this book may be reproduced or transmitted in any form
or by any means, electronic or mechanical, including photocopying, recording, or by
any information storage and retrieval system, without permission in writing from the
Publisher.

Twayne Publishers
An Imprint of Simon & Schuster Macmillan
1633 Broadway
New York, NY 10019-6785

Library of Congress Cataloging-in-Publication Data

Gerber, Philip L.
    Willa Cather / Philip Gerber. — Rev. ed.
        p. cm. — (Twayne's United States authors series ; no. 258)
    Includes bibliographical references.
    ISBN 0-8057-4035-X
    1. Cather, Willa, 1873-1947—Criticism and interpretation. 2. Women and litera-
ture—United States—History—20th century. I. Title. II. Series. III. Series:
Twayne's United States authors series ; TUSAS 258.
PS3505.A87Z645 1995
813' .52—dc20   94-45354
                                                                    CIP

The paper used in this publication meets the minimum requirements of American
National Standard for Information Sciences—Permanence of Paper for Printed Library
Materials. ANSI Z3948–1984. ∞ ™

10 9 8 7 6 5 4 3 2   (hc)

Printed in the United States of America

In memory of
Mildred R. Bennett

Contents

Publisher's Note

Willa Cather, Revised Edition by Philip Gerber draws on new materials and criticism made available since the 1975 publication of *Willa Cather*. Twayne Publishers is pleased to offer this revised critical study.

Preface to the Revised Edition

When the first edition of this book was composed, during the early 1970s, it seemed to me that a great deal of serious critical attention had been paid to Willa Cather. A fine biography had appeared, as well as a number of book-length studies of her work, and on the basis of her ongoing reputation she had been selected for inclusion in Jackson Bryer's *Fifteen Modern American Authors* (1969), a step serving to place her in a pantheon of her peers among twentieth-century writers. When, in 1973, Professor Bernice Slote of the University of Nebraska invited me to attend the international seminar on "The Art of Willa Cather," celebrating the centenary of Cather's birth and gathering together a host of scholars as well as others who had played important roles in Cather's life and career, such as her publisher, Alfred A. Knopf, the occasion provided, I thought, the capstone for the considerable appreciation of her writing that had accumulated during the three decades since her death. I tended to see the seminar as something of a finale, certainly not as a starting point.

I was scarcely prepared, then, for the dramatic upsurge of scholarly interest in Cather that got under way soon after my own volume on Cather was issued in 1975. During the two decades since then, an entirely new generation of Cather scholars has emerged. Among men and women alike, but increasingly, as time has gone on, among women, Cather's fiction has been examined from new points of view, some of them quite radical but all of them of value in establishing Cather's relevance to our own time.

Interest in Cather biography has been particularly lively, with an emphasis upon exploring the question of the novelist's sexual orientation and its possible impact upon her choice of fictional themes and characters as well as her manner of developing both. Part of my purpose in this revision is to deal with both of these strands of interest, to elucidate each so far as I find it possible to do so, without attempting to close off any line of argument or exploration, no matter how tempting the provocation.

A new arrangement of contents provides for the consideration of Cather's major contributions—her novels—by genre and chronologically, rather than thematically. A new emphasis is placed upon Cather's

short fiction, a separate chapter recognizing the stories as a major literary accomplishment in their own right. And I have attempted an
updating of the critical response to Cather's writing, reflective of the
upsurge of interest which has once again brought her to the fore among
American writers of the twentieth century.

Finally, it is my hope that this new volume will provide readers and
students with a credible overview of the contributions made by prominent Cather scholars, to assist in identifying the best of the new work,
both biographical and critical, and to point out the main lines of thought
that link the many investigations into Cather's life and work carried on
since the 1970s insofar as they seem to summarize the present state of
Cather studies and perhaps point the way to the future.

Philip Gerber
Brockport

Acknowledgments

In dedicating this revised edition to Mildred R. Bennett, I have intended to pay homage to her long efforts to establish Webster County, Nebraska, as an official "Catherland," efforts that have borne fruit to a degree that even Mrs. Bennett herself probably never imagined at the time she began to work toward that end. When she gave me my first, and very personal, tour of Cather's home territory some 30 years ago, Mrs. Bennett was full of unrealized dreams for the future, half-shaped plans that now largely have become reality. Every American writer should have a Mildred Bennett.

I wish to acknowledge also the vitality Patricia Phillips has brought to her role as Bennett's successor at the Willa Cather Pioneer Memorial and Education Foundation in Red Cloud. Her work with the Fifth International Willa Cather Seminar, held in Hastings, Nebraska, during the summer of 1993, demonstrated not only her vital enthusiasm for Cather but also the extent of her professional grasp of the critical approaches that need to be explored in maintaining the present high level of critical attention.

My attendance at this seminar, sponsored both by my own department and by the United University Professions of New York State, was of incalculable value as an aid to shaping the directions taken in this revision. I wish to acknowledge also the generous help of SUNY Brockport in supplying me with a travel grant that allowed me to read the otherwise inaccessible Cather letters held at a number of repositories, especially the Alderman Library, Charlottesville, Virginia; Duke University Library, Durham, North Carolina; the Huntington Library, San Marino, California; the Newberry Library, Chicago, Illinois; and the Pierpont Morgan Library, New York City. And finally, the Document Preparation Center on my home campus has, as always, provided me with expert help in the physical preparation of manuscript materials, both for Cather papers delivered at professional meetings and for this volume. At Twayne Publishers, Joseph M. Flora, General Editor of the United States Authors Series, and Mark Zadrozny, Senior Editor, have saved me from infelicities beyond count. To all of these people and groups, for all of their assistance, I am grateful.

Chronology

1873   Willa Cather born 7 December in Back Creek Valley, west of Winchester, Virginia.

1883   Moves with family to Webster County, Nebraska; resides at Catherton.

1884   Moves with family to Red Cloud, Nebraska.

1890   Graduates from high school in Red Cloud; enters University of Nebraska, Lincoln.

1893   Begins writing drama criticism for the *Nebraska State Journal*, Lincoln.

1895   Graduates from University of Nebraska; resides in Red Cloud and Lincoln.

1896   Moves in June to Pittsburgh as editor for *Home Monthly*.

1897   Summer residence in Nebraska; returns to Pittsburgh and post on *Pittsburgh Leader*.

1900–1901   First meeting with Isabelle McClung; winter of freelance writing in Washington, D.C.; returns to Pittsburgh.

1901–1903   Teaches Latin and English at Central High School, Pittsburgh; summer in Europe (1902) with Isabelle McClung.

1903–1906   Teaches English at Allegheny High School; *April Twilights* (1903); *The Troll Garden* (1905).

1906–1912   Joins *McClure's Magazine* in New York City (May); research trip to Boston (1907–08) for *McClure's* biography of Mary Baker Eddy; first meetings with Mrs. James T. Fields and Sarah Orne Jewett; resides in fall 1911 in Cherry Valley, New York; composes "Alexandra" and "The Bohemian Girl" (stories) and completes *Alexander's Bridge* (novel); leaves *McClure's* to devote herself to fiction.

1912   Publishes *Alexander's Bridge* and "The Bohemian Girl";

	visits Arizona; first contact with Anasazi cliff-dweller civilization.
1913	Publishes *O Pioneers!*; meets Olive Fremstad, model-to-be for Thea Kronborg; composes *The Song of the Lark*.
1914–1915	Resides in Pittsburgh; completes *The Song of the Lark*.
1915	Publishes *The Song of the Lark*; visits Mesa Verde and Taos.
1918	Publishes *My Ántonia*.
1920	Begins association with Alfred A. Knopf; publishes *Youth and the Bright Medusa*.
1922	Publishes *One of Ours*.
1923	*One of Ours* awarded Pulitzer Prize for 1922; publishes *A Lost Lady*.
1925	Publishes *The Professor's House*; edits the short stories of Sarah Orne Jewett; summer residence in New Mexico.
1926	Publishes *My Mortal Enemy*; provides introduction to Stephen Crane's *Wounds in the Rain*; summer residence in New Mexico while working on *Death Comes for the Archbishop*.
1927	Publishes *Death Comes for the Archbishop*.
1928	Visits Quebec; begins *Shadows on the Rock*.
1930	Awarded Howells Medal for fiction by the Academy of the National Institute of Arts and Letters.
1931	Publishes *Shadows on the Rock*.
1932	Publishes *Obscure Destinies*.
1933	Awarded Prix Femina Americain for *Shadows on the Rock*.
1935	Publishes *Lucy Gayheart*.
1936	Publishes *Not Under Forty*.
1937–1938	The Library Edition of Cather's collected works published by Houghton Mifflin.
1940	Publishes *Sapphira and the Slave Girl*.
1944	Awarded Gold Medal of the National Institute of Arts and Letters.
1947	Dies 24 April in New York City.

Chapter One

From the World to Nebraska

The old West, the old time,
The old wind singing through
The old, red grass a thousand miles.

Willa Cather, 1903

Taking our cue from biographer James Woodress that Willa Cather is a writer who more than most others "presents readers with the chance to compare biographical data with its transmutation into art,"[1] we begin with a sketch of her life. And that life, so far as it betokens the *writer*, may begin on a day in March 1883, when the Burlington Railroad deposited a Virginia family at its little station a mile from the settlement of Red Cloud, Nebraska. This was the Charles Cather party, at the end of its long journey into strange, unfamiliar territory. For American literature, the event was momentous, for it introduced to this yet untamed country the family's nine-year-old daughter, Willa, who later described her new home as being both her happiness and her curse. From her headlong encounter with it she was to produce the fiction that would win her an enduring place in American literary history.

In the years following the Civil War—that shock delivered to the American populace in 1861–65—the cry "Go west!" came as an answer to frustration and hard times for many southerners. This impulse established a need, and a host of new railroads proposed to fill it by carrying one and all into a new American Eden. In Nebraska, where the Burlington and Missouri River Railroad had been awarded immense tracts of land as an incentive to laying rails into new territory— Nebraska was only 16 years into statehood—buyers in quantity seemed ready to take up the lands the Burlington aimed at providing. Because the Union Pacific already crossed central Nebraska, the Burlington concentrated its efforts on the territories south of the Platte River, where competition was virtually nonexistent.

In preparation, the East was deluged with advertising that propagandized for the western movement. Millions of acres were offered for sale on easy terms. Even Canada and Europe were targets for the 100,000 territorial maps that described Nebraska as "a garden patch" and "a sea of wheat," with the best farming and stock-raising prospects in the world, ideal soil, water, and climate. So successful was the Burlington Railroad that by the end of 1872 it had unloaded more than 300,000 acres at $7.50 net an acre and was hauling 250,000 bushels of wheat each summer from Nebraska farms to Chicago markets.[2]

Spreading toward the Colorado mountains, the railroad hurriedly set up "towns" to serve as watering spots for steam locomotives and camps for section crews. Just as hastily, the towns were named, using alphabetical order—from Crete to Fairmont to Hastings to Juniata—so that in a sense the towns were there before their populations. Otherwise, Nebraska west of Lincoln was mostly raw prairie, mile upon mile of flat land, a plain of alluvial soil rolling 500 miles from east to west. The Burlington, merging with a small independent railroad in the Republican Valley, reached the hamlet of Red Cloud, and from that outpost the merging lines were joined by a spur running north and south between Red Cloud and Hastings. Thereby was opened an area of some 250,000 acres for settlement. "Go and See for Yourself. You will be Convinced, as Thousands have been Before you," advised the Burlington, hailing the new lands lying in the midst of what was described colorfully as the "Gulf Stream of Migration," an immense and largely imaginary utopia that grandiosely claimed as its border on the north the Aurora Borealis and on the south the Day of Judgment.[3]

As a family, the Cathers had established themselves in America during colonial times when Jasper Cather had come from Ireland. His greatgrandson was Charles Cather, who lived at the family's Virginia home, Willow Shade Farm, near Back Creek Valley in the hill country west of Winchester. On her maternal side, Willa Cather's forebears were also Virginian. Her grandmother, Rachel Seibert of Back Creek Valley, had married William Boak, a U.S. government official, had lived with him in Washington, and had borne him five children. At Boak's death, Rachel, then 38, returned to Back Creek Valley with her children. Among these was Mary Virginia Boak, who married Charles Cather on 5 December 1872. The newlyweds lived with Mrs. Boak, and their first daughter was born at her home a year later, on 7 December 1873. Christened Willela but usually called Willie among her family, she invented the name Willa for herself as she matured; and since her parents seem to have omitted a middle name, she eventually adopted that of the maternal line, spelling it Sibert. In standard nineteenth-century fashion, she was known as Willa Sibert Cather through the publication of her first four novels. But as the twentieth century came more fully into its own, she allowed herself to be known by the less formal name Willa Cather.

The first Cathers to settle in Nebraska were Willa's uncle and aunt, George Cather and his wife, Frances. They left Virginia for the West in 1873, shortly before their niece's birth, and by the time Willa was a year old they had established their homestead on a tract located between the Little Blue and Republican rivers, high ground that is familiar to readers of Cather stories as "the Divide." Because, however seductively it might be planned and plotted on railroad maps, the territory lacked settlements, roads, fences, or other reliable landmarks, life on the Divide was not easy. It was a treeless plain, essentially, overlaid with an undemarcated rug of shaggy reddish grass. The prairie winds blew continually, while the temperatures soared above 100 degrees Fahrenheit during the summers and plunged far below zero in the dark winters.

But the Cathers had come to stay. Their region soon was known by the unofficial title of Catherton. Willa's grandparents joined the Nebraska group, and this move allowed Charles and his family to move into the big house on Willow Shade Farm. Soon Willa's Grandmother Boak joined them, and for eight years they resided in the brick Virginia home, farming and raising sheep. By 1883 the family had grown to include Willa's younger brothers, Roscoe and Douglass, as well as her sister Jessica. Then the enormous sheep barn at Willow Shade burned to the ground, and this disaster seems to have tipped the balance. Willa's father, already feeling the tug of the West, disposed of the family property and farm equipment at auction and, with the $6,000 raised thereby, took his family west.[4]

Of all seasons, March was probably the most depressing time of the year to encounter Nebraska. The white mask of winter snow was melting away, but spring's greenery was not yet apparent. The flat land was at its bleakest then, perhaps, frozen solid if the cold lingered or sloggy with mud if the thaw was under way. Willa Cather, nine years old, was left with indelible impressions: sheet iron, that was what this land resembled, or it was naked, like the back of her hand. Excitement mingled with terror; it seemed as if she had wandered to the precipitous edge of the world. When her family left the railroad stop in an open Studebaker wagon pointed toward Catherton—a slow, jolting trip—the uninhabited territory gripped her. "I was sitting on the hay," she remembered, "holding on to the side of the wagon box to steady myself—the roads were mostly faint trails over the bunch grass in those days. The land was open range and there was almost no fencing. As we drove further and further out into the country, I felt a good deal as if we had come to the end of everything—it was a kind of erasure of personality."[5]

Charles Cather had told his daughter that a pioneer needed "grit," and on this bleak trip to Catherton she must have begun to comprehend what he meant. But after the family had settled on the Divide and during the 18 months they spent there, she was thoroughly impressed by the precise degree of spunk required of the settlers who poured in to make Webster County an outpost of the civilized world. Grandmother Boak, for example, found it essential to do her gardening armed with a hickory cane that was steel-tipped for killing the rattlesnakes that still nested in the area. To utilize the potentially rich cropland, a thick and tough covering of native sod had to be removed. With the help of a "breaking" plow, the sod peeled off like peat. Roots knotted together from decades of growth rendered the sod cohesive enough for use as "bricks" in building homes for the immigrants, its blocks providing thick walls that insulated against summer heat and also withstood winter gales. Some settlers lived in dugouts not much different from caves, and only the genuinely affluent could afford to haul in the expensive lumber necessary for a "regular" home. Fortunately, the Cather grandparents chose to return to Virginia for an extended visit, during which Charles and his family were able to occupy their wooden house.

Among the family's many surprises in this new territory was the discovery that native-born Americans were in the minority on the Divide. The Burlington's net had indeed been flung wide and far: as early as 1869, the railroad had planned for overseas distribution of Nebraska land pamphlets in English, German, Danish, and Scandinavian. Another distribution in 1873 added French- and Bohemian-language versions. During the 1870s, Nebraska's population grew by 310 percent, and it was no accident that foreign settlement comprised the majority of this growth. In fact, 23 nations were represented among the purchasers of Burlington land. In numbers, migrants from Bohemia led, followed by settlers coming from Denmark, Germany, Russia, and Sweden. These people left a deep impression on young Willa, who found their colonies "spread across [the] bronze prairies like the daubs of color on a painter's palette. . . . On Sunday we could drive to a Norwegian church and listen to a sermon in that language, or to a Danish or a Swedish church. We could go to the French Catholic settlement in the next county and hear a sermon in French, or into the Bohemian township and hear one in Czech, or we could go to church with the German Lutherans."[6] There were American-born settlers also, but for Willa Cather their settlements, lacking exotic color, did not so fully rouse her curiosity.

But the Europeans, with their distinctive national garb, odd tongues, and intriguing manners, were another matter. "I liked them from the first," said Cather, "and they made up for what I missed in the country." Wives, mothers, and daughters who had sacrificed homes overseas in order to pioneer a new continent were in a position to understand the Virginia child's hunger for the security she had left behind her in Shenandoah country. Cather gravitated to them for comfort, and they provided it. She took from these women also her first inklings of Old World values. On the pony her father put at her disposal, she followed buffalo trails across the prairie to visit the immigrant families and to hear their stories. Even if the conversations came to her in unfamiliar tongues, she forced herself to comprehend. "I have never," she said, "found any intellectual excitement any more intense than I used to feel when I spent a morning with one of those old women at her baking or butter making. I used to ride home in the most unreasonable state of excitement." And this statement was made during Cather's maturity, after she had been through the university, served as managing editor of a national magazine, visited many of the major cities of America, and traveled to Europe at least three times.[7]

With a child's natural instinct for exploration, Cather acclimated herself rapidly. If she tired of the dugouts and the soddies where so many of her foreigners lived, she had the buffalo wallows to investigate. The big herds were gone, slaughtered, but there remained depressions worn by their hooves and packed by their rolling until they held water as well as if they had cement bottoms. Meandering creeks where native cottonwoods tossed their glossy green leaves were magnets also; any genuine tree in this largely unwooded land became a valuable curiosity. And there were ravines that sunflowers filled with midsummer color; the remnants of old lagoons were golden with coreopsis. By the end of Cather's first autumn at Catherton, she was already looking at this shaggy-grass country with another pair of eyes. It was on the way to becoming her home. It had its terrifying aspects, but she had come to love its beauties as well. The land had gripped her attention, her emotions, with a passion she never escaped.

That early chapter in Cather's life in which she was free to come and go at will and to taste life fully on her own was ending. In the wide net cast by the railroad, many were caught who proved poorly suited to frontier conditions; not everyone could manage adjustment to the rough life of the Divide. Among those inadquately suited for the stringency of homesteading was Cather's own father, who found his new life considerably more precarious than he had anticipated. Catherton seemed hardly a place at all. The nearest medical care was 14 difficult miles away, and for the Cather children the three-month school term seemed most inadequate. On 11 September 1884, the Red Cloud newspaper announced: "Public sale of Charles Cather will be held 14 miles northwest of Red Cloud and 9 miles north of Invale, Section 22, Township 3, Range 11, on Monday, September 22."[8] Everything—cattle, horses, hogs, wagons, plows, machinery—was put on the block. The sale accomplished, Charles Cather prepared to go into business in Red Cloud.

When Willa Cather first lived there in 1884, Red Cloud was a prairie town of some 2,500 inhabitants, which meant that it was of considerable importance in that sparsely settled area. The immigrant strain was present there as well as in the countryside. That was not surprising, considering that as late as 1910 more than 900,000 of Nebraska's million-plus inhabitants were foreign-born. Only 14 years old, the town of Red Cloud was known already for its churches and schools. Webster Street's false-fronted wooden business structures, typical of frontier main streets, were being augmented by more permanent brick buildings. Plans were well under way for a two-story Opera House in which local organizations might gather for programs or road companies perform their dramas. With Red Cloud evolving into an important stop on the Burlington route to Denver, an Opera House seemed indispensable.

The Cathers found a house to rent at Third and Cedar streets, just off Webster. Not too well planned or built, the house was long and narrow, a story and a half in height. It had been constructed by a lumberman who, Willa Cather was always convinced, cared more for profit than for planning. She surmised that he had built on speculation, using second-hand and leftover pieces from his lumberyard. But the house was available and conveniently located, and the family moved in: parents; children; Grandmother Boak; Bess Seymour, who was Mrs. Cather's cousin; and the hired girl, Marjorie Anderson.[9] Two downstairs bedrooms in the cramped house were used by the parents and by Grandmother Boak, although Grandma's was scarcely worthy of the name bedroom, being no more than a screened-off portion of the kitchen. Upstairs, an unfinished "dormitory" accommodated the children. Later, when Willa was a teenager, a part of this upper floor was partitioned to form a private cubicle for her.

The most important fact, perhaps, was that the new house was located in a town with many civilized comforts, accessible education, adequate medical care, and easy contact with people. Willa became friends with the girls down the block, the Miners; their father ran a grand new brick establishment on Webster Street known as the Store. The four girls—Carrie, Irene, Margie, and Mary—offered Willa their friendship. And she, ever a leader, was soon casting them in plays composed by herself and performed in the Cather dormitory attic or in the Miner parlor. When Willa was 14, in 1888, her neighborhood troupe presented their play *Beauty and the Beast* downtown in the brand-new Opera House as a benefit for victims of that winter's historic blizzard.[10]

Whether staging one of her own playlets, reciting Longfellow's *Hiawatha* while dressed in Indian garb, or trekking the mile south to the depot to welcome one of the half-dozen stock companies that each winter played in Red Cloud now that the Opera House was open, Cather's instinct was to reach beyond the confines of the town, beyond the prairie, beyond Nebraska itself—to what, no one could yet suggest. Long after these girlhood days had passed, Carrie Miner Sherwood, with whom Cather had remained fast friends and regular correspondents, insisted that the girls were positive their neighbor would "go places"— not that they anticipated her writing career, specifically, "but we knew she would be *something* unusual, *something* special."[11]

The immigrants Willa Cather encountered in town were better educated, more "citified," and certainly more affluent than financially strapped sodbusters out on the Divide, but they were no less intriguing, no less valuable. The Miner girls' mother, for example, had been born in Norway, the daughter of an oboeist in the Royal Norwegian Orchestra. She was short, blond, stout, and—true to her childhood environment— a music lover. One of Cather's fond memories was of Mrs. Miner's fat little fingers skipping over the keyboard of her piano. And at one time she hired an itinerant musician to teach piano to her daughters, inspiring Mrs. Cather to employ him as well. Willa turned out to possess little native musical talent, and she never cherished an ambition for a career in music, but music remained a passionate lifelong interest. The Miner girls remained friends of hers for life.

Another local merchant, Charles Wiener, whose wife was French, possessed the most extraordinary private library in Red Cloud: French classics, the German edition of Scott's novels, and English translations of

Schiller. The Wieners conversed easily in French and German, and they inspired their young neighbor to learn French herself, not so much in order to join in their conversation, perhaps, as to read their books, for Willa had been allowed the run of their library.

"One of the people who interested me the most," Cather later said, was Annie Sadilek, the Bohemian hired girl who worked at the Miners'. Annie carried the spirit of the Divide into town, and she became for Cather the archetype of an open and life-loving human being whose spirit remained impervious both to the harsh life in the farmlands, where her father had recently died, and to her utter lack of means. Virtually without possessions, Annie apparently hungered for nothing. This fact, in a society already exhibiting a predilection for things, set Annie apart. Her life helped to persuade Cather that an individual can rise above circumstance, that one can to an extent create one's own conditions, and that happiness is decided ultimately by one's own capacity for enjoyment, beliefs that were to become important to her fiction.

At the Miners', Annie Sadilek became proficient at cooking and sewing, and eventually most of the clothes worn by her brothers and sisters back on the homestead came from her hands. Her family collected the small wages she earned, and if the Miners themselves had not held back enough to purchase her a pair of shoes, she would have continued wearing the oilcloth and denim slippers that she stitched for herself. To Willa, this free spirit was intriguing. She loved to loiter at the Miner home observing Annie's cheerful ways, admiring her boundless energy, and marveling at the phenomenon of an ignorant and penniless outlander becoming a magnet for the young men of Red Cloud. Reaching womanhood, Annie married a farmer and raised a large family on whom she lavished the same fullness of spirit. Over the years, Cather clung to this Bohemian girl and the values she represented.[12]

Other friends and acquaintances left permanent impressions also. One was Miss Evangeline King, principal of the South Ward School during the Cathers' second year in Red Cloud. "I wanted more than any thing else in the world to please her," said Willa, who relied on her guidance even after she was attending the high school. Later, Miss King was elected superintendent of public instruction for all of Webster County, in those times a most prestigious position, and eventually she joined the faculty of Kearney State Teachers College.

And there were the Garbers, illustrious citizens of Red Cloud in whose country home Cather was often a guest. Silas Garber had been among the founders of the town—it was his suggestion to name it after a famous chief of the Sioux Nation—and in 1873 he had been elected governor of the state. A widower, he had met a young beauty in California whom he had married and brought to the governor's mansion. Her youth and vivacity established her reputation as the most remarkable official hostess Lincoln had known. The gubernatorial term finished, the Garbers had returned to Red Cloud and their home in the cottonwood grove on a knoll just beyond town. Here Lyra Garber cared for her husband, who was a good deal older than she and had been injured in a carriage accident. Whenever health permitted, they entertained, and Cather appears to have been a welcome visitor at their home whenever they were not traveling. She remembered Lyra Garber as "a flash of brightness in a grey background," and the story of her romance with the governor, so distant from anything Cather herself was ever to experience, both enchanted and mystified her.[13]

Willa Cather grew to young womanhood enjoying such friends. She observed human nature with a keen eye, learning from everyone within her range, and she read widely in her home library and at the Wieners'. At age 14 she identified her hobbies as "Snakes & Sheakspear,"[14] in itself a good indication of the growing-up process she was passing through, a crew-cut, tomboy period when her ambition was to become a medical doctor. While engrossed with medicine, Cather thought surgery a likely specialty, and she began to practice for it by dissecting frogs and toads, which were abundant and easily caught. Such bloody activities raised a hue and cry of cruelty among the genteel of Red Cloud, but Cather did not relent. Instead, when the time came for her to graduate (one of three in the high school class of 1890!), she stood on the Opera House stage and formally compounded her "offense" by reciting an original oration defending open and free experimentation. Under her title, "Superstition versus Investigation," Willa asked the assembled citizens of Red Cloud to consider where the nation's future medical experts were to come from if novices in science were barred from proper instruction. For her, the life destroyed in experimentation since the beginning of time was as nothing compared with the large benefits that accrued from even a single great discovery, such as the circulation of the blood. The young who dissected the natural things surrounding them were not triflers, she insisted, nor were they cruel. On the contrary, she declared, "It is the most sacred right of man to investigate"; it is, further, "the hope of our age."[15]

This seems a remarkable salvo to be fired by one so young in 1890. And in a way it marked Cather's farewell not only to high school but to the town as well. She was eager to extend her horizons beyond Red

Cloud, and her first step toward this involved a 100-mile rail journey east to Lincoln, where she hoped to be accepted by the state university. She was just 16 years old.

Campus Years

The University of Nebraska in 1890 was little more than a motley collection of red brick buildings spaced on open, flat land. In the fashion of the times, pretentious Gothic and Romanesque towers adorned the four college structures, making them look disproportionately tall, especially when viewed against the newly planted saplings that stood in for trees. But Lincoln itself, with its population of 30,000, seemed a metropolis compared with Red Cloud. It lay on the main route of the Burlington, and to accommodate travelers and to serve those stopping over on government business, there were five hotels. For entertainment there were two theaters, each boasting a capacity in excess of 1,000.

Because the rudimentary Red Cloud schools did not yet furnish an adequate precollegiate education, Cather was unable to matriculate at once as a regular university student. Instead, she was assigned to a "prep" class for young people from the outlands. Sailing through her preparatory year, she became a full-fledged freshman in the fall of 1891. Hers was a tiny beginning class, and the entire university enrolled fewer than 400 students. But all things being relative, for Cather the campus was huge and magic, a true wonderland led by professors whose wide learning and varied abilities promised that new and exciting windows on the world were about to be opened.

A young English instructor, Herbert Bates, just out of Harvard University, brought to the campus the attractive aura of the East. He helped Cather publish her first serious writing ventures. An ROTC lieutenant, John J. Pershing, was destined to lead the American Expeditionary Force in World War I. Chancellor James Canfield, who had been attracted from Kansas and would later head Ohio State University, was newly arrived, along with his daughter Dorothy, who joined the student body. As Dorothy Canfield Fisher she would become a writer and be awarded the Pulitzer Prize in fiction. Willa Cather and Dorothy became fast friends; the world seemed to be opening up for her in many attractive directions.

While at the university, Willa Cather made her first tentative moves toward a writing career. Two campus literary magazines, the *Lasso* and the *Hesperian*, were her training ground. She broke into print early and rather unexpectedly when an essay written during her freshman year so impressed her instructor, Ebenezer Hunt, that he arranged to have it printed in the *Nebraska State Journal*, a leading local newspaper. Within a few months, the *Journal* took a second Cather essay, "Shakespeare and Hamlet."

Simultaneously, Cather was trying her hand at fiction. As she grew into middle age she was prone to disown these early attempts, to pretend they didn't exist, and to do whatever she could to prevent their being unearthed from old files and reprinted. But she was candid in 1921, telling a journalist that the college magazine had once printed "several of my perfectly honest but very clumsy attempts to give the story of some of the Scandinavian and Bohemian settlers who lived not far from my father's farm. In these sketches, I simply tried to tell about the people, without much regard for style."[16]

The first of these was called "Peter" and is what Cather called it, a sketch, a reminiscence of a local suicide colored by youthful imagination. Peter Sadelack is a violinist from Prague who never should have attempted to settle in Nebraska, but, like Cather's father, did so. He is incapacitated by a stroke, and his son Antone manages the homestead while Peter drinks his sorrows away. Provoked by his son and wife's threats to sell his violin (which he cannot use since his paralytic stroke), Peter smashes the beloved instrument rather than see it sold, then kills himself in a gruesome manner with a shotgun. Even before the funeral, however, Antone is on his way to town to sell the violin bow that Peter had neglected to break. *Bald* and *emotional* were the adjectives the mature Cather used in dismissing this tale, and they suit it admirably. But "Peter" is significant in revealing Cather's first writerly instincts: to set down in unmistakable detail something about the harshness of immigrant life on the Nebraska Divide. That theme became important in Cather's fiction, and "Peter" is its first expression.

Cather's teacher Herbert Bates helped her to submit "Peter" to a little magazine in Boston called the *Mahogany Tree*. Wonder of wonders for a neophyte writer just 18 years old—it was accepted. Willa Cather, university student, was a published author of fiction! The editors of the campus magazine the *Hesperian* were impressed and requested permission to reprint "Peter." It appeared one month after the magazine published a second story Cather had submitted. This was "Lou, the Prophet," concerning a Danish immigrant, and just as unrelentingly grim as "Peter" had been. Lou's life is said to be "as sane and uneventful as the life of his plowhorses, and [just] as thankless."[17] Facing the loss of his crops in a withering drought, Lou becomes deranged, and in a state of mad belief that God somehow is punishing him, he disappears, drowned perhaps in the shallow remains of the river, his body trapped by quicksand.

Failure, despair, insanity, violence: these were strong themes, and in later work Willa Cather would handle them with greater art. But it seems significant that at an early stage she was not shying away from some of the stark truths concerning the lives she had witnessed.

In Lincoln, campus publications provided Willa Cather with a meager enough stage on which to perform but one that was sufficient to her needs until her junior year, when she received a proposal from the local newspaper, the *Nebraska State Journal*. How would she like to contribute a regular column? Accepting with enthusiasm, she composed local-color sketches that reflected her curiosity about the life around her, and soon she was given the more challenging assignment of reviewing theatrical productions in the Lincoln theaters. In December 1893 a rival paper had condemned local dramatic criticism as no more than "a dreary waste of undiluted mediocrity" tossed off by writers who lacked the standards essential to making significant judgments.

Willa Cather soon changed all that. It was not long before theatrical troupes stopping in Lincoln were aware that nothing short of their very best performances would be acceptable; anything less would invite caustic words from the *Journal*'s new and very young woman critic. Two years of Cather's weekly drama column, which she called "The Passing Show," earned her a reputation sufficiently widespread to cause the *Des Moines Register* to comment that Lincoln enjoyed the best theatrical criticism in the West.[18]

Nebraska lay at an immense distance from New York City, the heart of American stage activity; and Broadway standards could become Cather's only in her imagination: she had never seen a play outside of Nebraska, let alone on Broadway. Nonetheless, she never hesitated to judge rigorously when she suspected that a traveling company was sloughing off just because it was appearing in the boondocks. When Rider Haggard's fantasy *She* came to town, Cather castigated both play and players. Its hero, Edwin Brown, was "corpulent and stagy," and she said so: "he could not even read his lines intelligently." The heroine herself was "quite pretty—when she had her veil on"; but the actress, like her costar, "was utterly incapable of reading her lines." The play itself was damned as being "as awful as the people who played it."[19] The managing editor of the *Journal*, Will Owen Jones, declared that the fierce Miss Cather threw a scare into actors from coast to coast. Players visiting Lincoln slept poorly, never knowing what new critical assault to expect from "that meatax young girl."[20]

Of significance here was that Cather was beginning to become engrossed with the possibility of flawless artistry. When a performance called for it, she could praise as lavishly as she could condemn. Of Richard Mansfield's performance as Beau Brummell, she commented that one was left with little to say when faced by real art. Of a perfect work, she felt certain, no one but a fellow artist was qualified to speak of the how or the why. Here the young Cather can be seen testing her own wings, reaching for an ideal, determined to soar, and setting the highest standards for herself.

She formed a great attachment to Edgar Allan Poe, who never let the flag of his art be sullied. That Poe could be a liar and an egoist mattered not at all to Cather, for the man was nothing, his work, everything: "There is so little perfection." All that mattered to her was that Poe had preserved the ideal of perfect work. "I have wondered so often how he did it," Cather said in her graduation speech before the university literary societies. "How he kept his purpose always clean and his taste always perfect." In 1895 she had no answer to her question; she needed to live the life of art for herself in order to confirm what she had said about Poe.[21]

Chapter Two
From Nebraska to the World

You must know the world before you can know the village.

Sarah Orne Jewett to Cather, 1908

By the time Willa Cather graduated from the University of Nebraska in 1895, she had earned a journalistic reputation in Lincoln and even beyond the borders of the state. The weekly *Lincoln Courier* invited her to join its staff on a part-time basis, and soon she was writing both for it and for the *Journal*. Her hopes were high. The *Nebraska Editor* cited her as one certain to become known on a wide scale, and the *Weekly Express* in Beatrice, Nebraska, identified her as a writer soon to have national acclaim.[1] During this period, Cather lived in Red Cloud and mailed her work to the newspapers, traveling to Lincoln only on visits or to cover the theatrical season. It became apparent to her, however, that she would never fulfill such predictions in this manner, lacking full-time employment in Lincoln and feeling that life in Red Cloud was something comparable to Siberian exile.

Even so, any significant forward movement for her had to wait until spring 1896 and an offer of employment from a small Pittsburgh magazine, the *Home Monthly*, which Cather accepted eagerly. The writing she did for *Home Monthly* was of the fleeting variety, but there was plenty of it to keep her busy. When the magazine's owner, Charles Axtell, employed her, he intended that she serve as a jack-of-all-trades, and she soon found herself writing most of the copy. Not that she minded all that much, for if she was writing trivia, she at least was writing full-time. One natural compensation occurred to her at once: she could use the *Home Monthly* as an outlet for her own sketches and stories.

Cather began soon to insert her fiction among the magazine's otherwise quite mundane columns. The August 1896 issue carried two of her tales of Nebraska. One of them, "Tommy, the Unsentimental," indicates a new attitude toward the Divide, her fear of its hostile environment being mitigated by a maturing appreciation of its wild attractiveness. The contrived love-story plot of "Tommy" occurs on a summer day when the sun of "hot brass" and a searing wind from the south have produced the "sickening, destroying heat" that Willa knew so well from Augusts spent in the Catherton area. Yet the heroine, recently returned from school in the East, finds that she is "mighty homesick" for Nebraska's huge blue sky, its vast plains, and even "this hateful, dear old, everlasting wind."[2] So there was something good at last, it seemed, about the midland frontier; but apparently Cather had to leave the West in order to appreciate it.

Pittsburgh

In Pittsburgh Cather was impressed less by the stranglehold the steel kings exerted on civic affairs generally than by the cultural life their great wealth had made possible. This was, after all, her first experience of living in a large city, and she reveled in her new opportunities. So many of the great names in music and the theater performed in Pittsburgh, and at Carnegie Hall a continual round of recitals and concerts took place. Using as leverage her experience on the Lincoln newspapers, Cather was able to establish herself with the *Pittsburgh Leader* as a part-time drama critic. Her reviews now served double duty, for she mailed many of them back to Lincoln, where her "Passing Show" column continued to run. Soon she moved to a full-time job with the *Leader* as assistant telegraph editor, which required routine editing of out-of-town news coming in on the wire services. Having a daytime work schedule left her free to attend to the theater at night and to socialize. Her critical status broadened to encompass musical functions and book reviewing.

Socially, Cather found herself much in demand, with several men friends expressing an interest. This was a new and flattering turn, but Cather seems never to have entertained much serious notion of marrying. Elizabeth Moorhead, who first met Cather in Pittsburgh in 1905 and knew her quite well there, said her first impression was that Cather "was a person who couldn't easily be diverted from her chosen course," which was to make a career for herself.[3] Indeed, a strong preference for remaining single already was apparent during her university years, and it seems to have become a conscious life decision during the prime marriageable years directly following university graduation. From that period, even in her transitory reviews, she speaks much of art and its stringent demands upon the individual who cares passionately. Cather's decision to be first, last, and always a writer merely strengthened with the passage of time. In her thinking, marriage was incompatible with a career, at least for a woman at the turn of the twentieth century. The dire consequences of ignoring this unpleasant reality and acting as if the situation were any different are portrayed throughout Cather's fiction, in which marriage for an artist exists but is never truly satisfying or very successful.

The tight circle of Cather's friends in Pittsburgh was drawn chiefly from people who shared her artistic interests or were themselves bent upon artistic careers. Dorothy Canfield's father had moved to Ohio State University in Columbus, not too far away for Dorothy to visit Cather in Pittsburgh at intervals, and their friendship deepened. Cather met George Siebel, a young writer who had musical interests and whose cosmopolitan family was the type toward which she naturally gravitated. The Siebels were of German extraction but were devotees of French literature. They entertained Cather at their home on a weekly basis. Good home-cooked German food, good French readings in Gustave Flaubert, Victor Hugo, Théophile Gautier—who could want more than this? So close to this family did Cather become that she regularly spent her Pittsburgh Christmases with them.

After serving her journalistic apprenticeship in Pittsburgh, Cather probably would have been wise to abandon the Steel City as soon as humanly possible. In retrospect, it seems probable that, had she proceeded at once to New York City, her writing career might have blossomed sooner. But she stayed in Pittsburgh for 10 years, held there by a certain reserve, a measure of insecurity, and perhaps also because life was made so seductively pleasant by activities and friends. The city seemed a good place to live in, she wrote her friend Will Owen Jones, and 1900 was shaping up as the happiest year in her life.[4]

Free Board at the McClungs'

During the winter of 1900–1901, Cather attempted a break with Pittsburgh, but her new job, translating for a government office in Washington, proved a mistake from the start. In February she wisely left Washington but—unwisely—went not to New York but back to Pittsburgh. She may well have been influenced in this decision by the security offered by a new friend.

In 1899 Cather had made the acquaintance of Isabelle McClung, the beautiful daughter of a Pittsburgh judge. The McClungs, well off financially, inhabited a world Cather had never known: a mansion staffed by servants, an address on fashionable Murray Hill near the Monongahela, a gracious style of living that included much leisure. The young ladies' mutual attraction to things theatrical was what first drew them together—Cather had met Isabelle in an actress's dressing room—and a deep camaraderie soon came about, one in which Isabelle served as that individual "every writer needs most, the helping friend."[5] The elder McClungs being persuaded by their daughter to invite Cather to stay in their spacious home, she accepted and lived with them for five years. Simultaneously, she gave up journalism in order to embark on another wrong track, teaching Latin at Central High School, then teaching English, and remaining until 1905, when she transferred to Allegheny High School across the river.

The dominant picture that emerges of Cather during the years following 1900 is of an eager and aspiring but somewhat frustrated young writer who was struggling to muster the courage it would take to devote herself wholly to a literary career. An almost unendurable tension was building as a result. Being free of serious personal entanglements or responsibilities, Cather was free to go where and when she pleased. Yet she remained in Pittsburgh, bound to her teacher's desk, attempting to balance antagonistic career strands. What held her back from taking the essential, all-or-nothing plunge into a different and untested life pattern seems to have been a deeply seated need for the security offered by her situation in Pittsburgh, as well as a lingering doubt as to whether she could succeed as a writer on the national scene.

At the McClungs', Cather was made very comfortable, much too comfortable for her own good, possibly. Everything was arranged to facilitate her extra-teaching career as a fiction writer. The room she and Isabelle shared lay at the back of the house, overlooking the garden and the sloped lawn leading to the Monongahela. It was a classic retreat of greenery, with many splendid trees, and no close neighbors disturbed the friends' sense of privacy. For Willa's writing, a third-story sewing room was transformed into a study. Far from the family bustle on the lower floors, she was able to enjoy the solitude on which creativity thrives.

Aside from an occasional free evening when neither a play nor a concert was scheduled, Cather's weekends were her own, a time when no attention need be paid to anything but the stories and poems that teased her mind. Even Isabelle's Sunday-afternoon literary teas were not allowed to intrude on Cather's privacy. The temptation to join the guests downstairs was powerful, since faculty members from the Carnegie Tech drama and music departments were regularly present, as were members of Isabelle's Dante Society. But Cather—a kind of "writer in residence"—usually declined. "She would be at her desk in the attic leagues away . . . in that rich world of imagination," Elizabeth Moorhead report-ed. "Sunday afternoons should be kept for her own work [and] she must let nothing interfere."[6]

To leave Pittsburgh would necessarily mean a break with Isabelle McClung. This was a separation Cather clearly dreaded. Always given to feeling rather desperately in need of friendship, she had never felt so close to another person as she did to Isabelle, so close, indeed, that years later, in 1916, when Isabelle announced her impending marriage, Cather found herself unable to start the new novel she had scheduled because of her fear that Isabelle's marriage would mean the end of their special rela-tionship—a relationship that in recent years has become the storm cen-ter of a good deal of biographical controversy.[7]

Europe

Not being required to contribute toward her room and board at the McClung home, Cather was able to save enough from her salary to pay for a first trip abroad in 1902, with Isabelle as her companion. This voy-age was an adventure long anticipated. The young women headed first for England, where they visited the poet A. E. Housman, for whose *A Shropshire Lad* Cather had developed great enthusiasm. When Dorothy Canfield joined them in London, the young women crossed the channel to France, landed at Dieppe, and then proceeded to Rouen, Paris, and then southern France.

Halfway around the globe from Nebraska, France had long existed in Cather's imagination as being a totally new and strange world. It had been thought of as a thing altogether different from anything she had ever known, and so she was amazed by the reality of seeing near Barbizon wheat fields that were every bit as flat as those of Nebraska. Her notions concerning Nebraska's uniqueness needed revamping; the world was not after all so very different. Cather was beginning to under-stand her home place better for having seen something of the wide world beyond its borders.

In Europe Cather satisfied two needs, but neither was ever made explicit, and both were most likely unconscious. Her strong ties with things foreign, first established during her girlhood on the Divide, were revitalized when she saw for herself the continent from which her immi-grants had sailed to new lives. At the same time, everything she saw of the world at large brought her an improved perspective on her own native postage stamp of land. What Nebraska signified was now more fully comprehended, and this greater understanding prepared Cather for a major fictional expression of the state and its diverse population in her novels and stories.

First Books

These tales were not being written in 1902, and they were not to be written until Cather ceased subordinating her writing to her employment. At her age—she turned 30 in 1903—major works should have been under way, but her energy-draining classroom duties and the planned schedule of social life at the McClungs' were not conducive to writing novels. Even so, a persistent urge to produce solid work of some magnitude was apparent. To be published in a magazine, which once had given her such a thrill, no longer satisfied; it seemed now almost as ephemeral as a newspaper appearance. Something more permanent was demanded, something more concrete; something hefty to hold in the hands, carry about, set on a shelf; something with more of its own identity, an artifact that would neither perish as suddenly as an actor's performance nor be buried among the works of others in a throwaway daily sheet. In short, she experienced an irresistible drive to write a book. And within three years of returning from Europe, she produced two.

Not surprisingly, the first books to carry the Cather name were collections. She had been interested in writing verse since her college days, and poems could be worked on in the brief hours available to her outside of the classroom. In 1903 she collected a group of these poems under the title *April Twilights* and subsidized the book's publication by Richard Badger. As poetry, Cather's volume was not a great one, perhaps not even a genuinely promising one. But as a step in her literary evolution, the book served its purpose; for *April Twilights*, with its impressive Boston imprint, brought her some measure of local fame and a degree of notice on a wider scale.

At their poorest, the poems fell into wholly conventional lines indistinguishable from the verses of a host of aspirants. Reflecting the current literary and artistic fashions, classical Greek and Roman themes predominated. Other poems, such as "London Roses" and "Poppies on Ludlow Castle," though lyrical attempts to respond to Cather's European visit, slavishly imitated her hero Housman:

> Lads and their sweethearts lying
>   In the cleft of the windy hill;
> Hearts that are hushed of their sighing,
>   Lips that are tender and still.[8]

The largest group of poems evoked nature in bursts of feeling; some, however finely drawn, remained traditional themes traditionally expressed. Among all of Cather's 24 verses, only one poem in any way truly suggested the author of *O Pioneers!* or *My Ántonia*. The briefest verse of all did provide at least a glimpse of what was to come. In eight lines of blank verse, "Prairie Dawn" managed to establish a clear link with details of Cather's Nebraska past:

> A crimson fire that vanquishes the stars;
> A pungent odor from the dusty sage;
> A sudden stirring of the huddled herds;
> A breaking of the distant table-lands
> Through purple mists ascending, and the flare
> Of water-ditches silver in the light;
> A swift, bright lance hurled low across the world,
> A sudden sickness for the hills of home.[9]

Cather's second book—also a collection—was more portentous, a volume of stories issued under an obscurely allusive title, *The Troll Garden*, with epigraphs from Christina Rossetti and Charles Kingsley.[10] Among its seven tales are superb examples of the short story rarely surpassed either by Willa Cather herself or by other Americans. This fact might not have been immediately apparent to readers of 1905, for the gems of this collection were scattered among trivialities. Cather was riding the crest of a grand passion for the work of Henry James, in her opinion "the perfect writer";[11] and ever since the 1890s, she had been influenced by his stories of artists, their dedication to their work, their tribulations, and their rewards. Consequently, the bulk of her *Troll Garden* stories concerned artists.

Three stories are far superior to those derivative of James, and these look forward to Cather's mature writings. "Paul's Case," which approaches the question of artistry from the viewpoint of a boy utterly without talent but hopelessly deluded into believing he can nourish himself through life as a hanger-on, seems by all odds the superior story. A finished product, it is genuine in its approach and is written in clean, simple prose. For years it served as Cather's most anthologized selection. Two others, only slightly less perfect, perhaps, especially as concerns form, owe their existence directly to the author's Nebraska background. Both "A Wagner Matinee" and "The Sculptor's Funeral" confront the impossibility of achieving artistic fulfillment on a frontier where practical needs overwhelm all other considerations. These stories project Cather's fundamental problem in her postuniversity years: the tension between the realistic need to support herself and the emotional urge to dedicate her life to her art.

Life under the Volcano

By 1903 Willa Cather had composed the stories in *The Troll Garden* and was long overdue for her break with Pittsburgh. But she seemed in a state of psychological paralysis that prevented her from abandoning her established routine. Then a "fortunate accident" occurred—a chain of circumstances that brought her work to the attention of S. S. McClure, the publisher of America's fastest growing magazine. *McClure's* rocketing circulation had been stimulated by aggressive muckraking articles produced by a stable of talented, crusading journalists, and McClure was ever on the lookout for additional writers who showed promise.

Hearing Cather's work praised, McClure spontaneously wrote her a personal note inviting her to submit for consideration in his magazine any stories she might have on hand. Thrilled—shocked also, most likely—to receive unsolicited encouragement from one of the brightest lights in publishing, Cather responded with a group of recently completed tales; and McClure, who was prone to sudden enthusiasms, professed to see in them a very real basis for a book-length collection.

Acting on his hunch, McClure telegraphed Cather in Pittsburgh and proposed that she come to New York for an interview. She did so, and during that session her life became a totally new proposition. She walked into the *McClure's* building feeling that she was not anything of particularly great value, but when she came out, she knew that her worth had soared. The salient clue was to be found in her changed attitude toward the city's busy streetcars; where previously she had paid them little heed, now she found herself taking extra caution lest one strike her and end a life so greatly worth saving.[12]

The dynamic personality of S. S. McClure himself had worked this miraculous change—Cather was certain of that. His charisma was powerful. He was a man for whose sake followers would willingly be burned at the stake, of that she was convinced. During their first interview, McClure won Cather's heart when, on learning that some of her fiction had already been rejected by his magazine, he called the readers to his office, demanding that they account for their poor stewardship. For Cather this was a moment to savor. As a spectator, she sat watching the confrontation, her chin held high, and thought her hour had struck. McClure took her stories, the same that earlier had been spurned, and to her surprise required not a single change. He fairly brimmed with plans to make something important of her.[13]

S. S. McClure was a man who so erupted with original ideas that he reminded his employee Ray Stannard Baker of a live volcano. Too excitable ever to stand still, he was forever rushing off on field trips in search of new subjects and new writers. These forays might take him to outposts of the Far West or across the Atlantic to Europe and Africa, and they resulted in heaps of manuscripts and scores of major plans. In his absence, McClure's staff could proceed with some equanimity to edit the magazine until the calm was broken again by the boss's return. Trouble brewed perennially in the offices, McClure's writers chafing against his continual changes of plans. He wanted the fun," said Ida Tarbell understandingly, "of seeing his finds quickly in print." According to Lincoln Steffens, he ran a dictatorship, albeit a benevolent one: "He could raise a rumpus" when thwarted by his employees.[14]

McClure could scarcely hope to hold the lid down on this boiling pot. Inevitably, there was an explosion. Intraoffice politics became bitter; the staff considered leaving the magazine en masse and starting a journal of their own. Eventually they did, in a wholesale desertion that precipitated a crisis. McClure had to form a new editorial group at once or perish. As he searched for capable individuals at present unattached, he thought of his new discovery in Pittsburgh, and Cather found herself in receipt of an astounding offer: would she leave Pittsburgh to come work for *McClure's* in New York? She would; for her it came as the opportunity of a lifetime.

Because the offer arrived in May, it was only a matter of days before school would close for the summer and Cather could accept, rushing to New York to be swept into the roaring current known as *McClure's*. In 1905 Cather had spent a week as McClure's guest in New York; "now here she was again, obedient to his summons, but a little uncertain as to what was expected of her."[15] She soon learned. McClure had very definite ideas of an editor's duties, and an editor was not long in understanding that creative editing was something done in the field only, never at a desk in a comfortable room. As soon as Cather's orientation had been accomplished, McClure put a most important assignment into her hands and gave her a railroad ticket. In his search for items to tickle the public palate, he had chanced upon a lengthy manuscript by Georgine Milmine. It was far from the most perfect writing in the world, but its subject matter—Mary Baker Eddy and her Christian Science movement, just then reaching the peak of their influence—seemed surefire for an exposé of the *McClure's* type. Milmine's provocative but slipshod book was being readied for use as a major serial; and at *McClure's*, accuracy was paramount. The magazine was used to handling red-hot issues, and it tried to present them incontrovertibly. But a number of errors had been detected already in the Milmine manuscript, and the only solution seemed to be for trustworthy Willa Cather to take the problem in hand. She would need to work on location at the heart of the Christian Science movement, and doing so meant traveling to Boston for as long a stay as the job might require.

House of Memories

Not long after her arrival in Boston in 1908, Cather was invited to visit the widow of the famous publisher James T. Fields at her home. It proved to be one of the truly momentous visits in Cather's life. A sense of history permeated the Fields drawing room, whose hostess herself seemed miraculously to "reach back to Waterloo." From her personal recollections, Mrs. Fields could speak of Cather's idol Henry James and of his earliest efforts at composition, of Robert and Elizabeth Browning and their life in Italy, of her dinner party in Dickens's honor at which Dr. Oliver Wendell Holmes had spoken of actors "in a way that quite disturbed Longfellow." On every hand "that house of memories," as Cather remembered it, was stocked with mementos, which included a lock of John Keats's hair.[16]

The Fields home was more than a mere sanctuary from a too rapidly changing world, for Mrs. Fields introduced Cather to a living writer who became a decisive influence on her career.[17] So it was not Mrs. Fields who became the central attraction on Cather's first afternoon at 148 Charles Street but Sarah Orne Jewett, who was a guest the same day Cather visited. In 1908 the author of *Deephaven* and *The Country of the Pointed Firs* stood in the first ranks of the local-color realists. From her, Willa would learn the secrets of her chosen profession. She had long recognized that Jewett's stories of Maine and its people offered something quite apart from the depressing round of "machine-made historical novels" and "dreary dialect stories" that dominated contemporary fiction. In Jewett she recognized a writer of unimpeachable integrity who concentrated her efforts on the region she knew most intimately, who refused to strive unduly for flashy effects, and who, rather than concocting a trumped-up pseudodialect to humor her readers, used her native idiom, "the finest language any writer can have."[18]

Jewett responded to Cather with the gift of friendship, and during one of their many talks the two were commenting upon a recent magazine story about a mule; the story's claim to fame appeared to center on the fact that its rural author had been simply and solely a mule driver. The story itself struck both women as being hopelessly limited, parochial, and ungrammatical. Jewett summarized for her new, young friend: "You must know the world before you can know the village."[19] Cather committed the remark to memory and quoted it often. More important, she applied it to herself and to her attitude toward the youthful materials that soon emerged anew as ideas for her novels. Her years away from Nebraska and all she had seen and heard in Pittsburgh, New York, Europe, and Boston were contributing toward an increased broadening of her perspective concerning the flat lands of home. At last she was able to see Nebraska through a new set of eyes.

The Cather-Jewett friendship lasted only 16 months, for the older writer died the following year. But the two had corresponded regularly; and in one of her notes Jewett included a second sentence that became axiomatic to Cather: "The thing that teases the mind over and over for years, and at last gets itself put down rightly on paper—whether little or great, it belongs to Literature."[20] There were youthful materials—scenes, characters, anecdotes, themes—that since her university days Cather had been attempting to record *rightly*. Her efforts to date seemed to her shamefully experimental, amateurish, and awkward; but with a volition of their own, these same memories persisted in urging themselves as usable themes: life on the Nebraska Divide, and the struggle of the gifted individual to achieve—these were two of them.

Toward the Novel

As Cather's tenure at *McClure's* lengthened into years, her heavy editorial duties worked to smother her own writing. She produced assigned pieces for the magazine: major articles on the arts and summary reviews of the drama, opera, and ballet seasons. S. S. McClure, who in 1907 had turned 50, wished to publish the story of his rags-to-riches life. Always an idea man rather than a writer, he prevailed upon Cather, now his managing editor, to ghost his autobiography; and she, grateful to the person who had brought her from the obscurity of a high school class-room to the forefront of American journalism, could not decline. Her genuine affection for McClure made the assignment a labor of love, and no author credit was expected or given. But McClure, both in magazine serialization and in book form, preceded his life story with a special acknowledgment of his debt to Cather.[21]

The year 1912 marked the sixth year of Cather's editorship. The thrill of connection with a leading magazine had dimmed; the excitement of a first plunge into metropolitan life had given way to a more sober reflection. At *McClure's* Cather had solidified new friendships with Edith Lewis and Elizabeth Shepley Sergeant, both of whom after her death wrote memoirs of her. She attended the opera regularly, she had satisfied her thirst for good theater, and she had been introduced to notable after notable. She had traveled extensively, more than once to Europe. But none of this sufficed for what was missing; whatever she was doing seemed only second best and not what was ultimately intended for her.

In making a final break with the magazine world, Cather was strengthened in her resolve by Sarah Orne Jewett. The older writer had adopted her as a protégée and in her last months shared the wisdom she had accumulated during a long life. She gently guided Cather toward goals that seemed important. Having read Cather's story "On the Gull's Road," she praised it in a letter that also said, "It makes me the more sure that you are far on your road toward a fine and long story of very high class." The gentle nudge toward the novel form comes through clearly if subliminally. "The Sculptor's Funeral" had marked Cather's highest achievement, Jewett felt, and more in that precise vein was indicated: "You have your Nebraska life," she reminded her, an asset of incalculable value.[22]

In Jewett's opinion, the crucial thing to consider was whether Cather's mundane writing at the magazine could be allowed to continue if her deepest creative abilities were ever to mature. The big question to ask was whether five years hence Cather might be writing things finer in any way than she was writing at present: "This you are anxiously saying to yourself!" And Cather undoubtedly was asking this precise question, for she was convinced that she possessed something uncommon.[23]

With great tact, Jewett suggested the painful fact that Willa Cather was approaching her middle years without having produced work of substantial scope. "When one's first working power has spent itself," she cautioned, "nothing ever brings it back." Jewett asked Cather to consider a hypothetical instance—to suppose that the year 1908, rather than having been spent in Boston and in long office hours bringing order to the Milmine articles—had instead been spent on "three or four stories" of the caliber of "The Sculptor's Funeral." The truth behind this speculation was something Cather could not easily dismiss.[24]

Making the Break

By 1911, after procrastinating for far too long, Cather was prepared to ease out of *McClure's* and to drive toward the "quiet centre" Jewett had prescribed. Accordingly, in June Cather went to Jewett's girlhood home in South Berwick, Maine, and found it, as she had hoped, the one spot on earth where she could gain a perfect rest. Maine was a fine, isolated place in which to achieve a perspective on her career, to decide what was right and possible for her. Elizabeth Sergeant, who had obtained a copy of *The Troll Garden*, wrote to say how much she liked the stories in it. But Cather replied that not much in these early tales seemed truly good to her now—not even in the Nebraska stories, which she now thought ruined by a petulant attitude she had been unable to keep from expressing in those days when she had felt chained unfairly to the West and barred from all the things she really wanted to do, years when she feared it really might be her destiny to die in a cornfield.

As fall began, Cather took a leave of absence from *McClure's* and, with Isabelle McClung, went to Cherry Valley in the Finger Lakes area of New York, where the two rented a house. In this rural setting of hills, quiet waters, and crimson autumn maples, peaceful now with the summer people departed, Cather at last was free to work, and she wrote unstintingly. She had already created a book-length piece of fiction and had most of it down on paper. Her first order of business at Cherry Valley was to complete this story and to arrange for its serialization in *McClure's* the following spring. The book became, as she later referred to it, her first "first-novel."[25] Since she still idolized Henry James as the commanding personage in American letters, *Alexander's Bridge* is highly Jamesian in its symmetry of form and its engrossing interest in relationships between people of an artistic bent. Through editor Ferris Greenslet, her friend since their meeting during her visit to Boston, she managed to secure a contract for book publication by his firm, Houghton Mifflin.

Gathering momentum, Cather composed another story, a long one, "The Bohemian Girl," which then was scheduled to appear in *McClure's* after her novel concluded its serialization. "The Bohemian Girl" was of an entirely different stamp from her novel, which was set in London for the most part and concerned artists. In contrast, "The Bohemian Girl" opens on a transcontinental express as it swings down the winding track of the Sand River Valley headed west. In the observation car sits a young man relishing "the fierce sunlight which beat in upon his brown face and neck and strong back."[26] Nils Ericson's return to the Nebraska Divide is essentially Cather's own surrender to her more natural materials. She continued in this vein with another long tale of the Divide. It opens on a day in the early 1880s among a "cluster of low drab buildings huddled on the gray prairie, under a gray sky," a scary scene etched into her mind from her early memories of infinitesimal Bladen, Nebraska, not far from the Catherton settlement.[27] This story she called "Alexandra." Not published at once, it waited to serve instead as the opening portion of the longer work *O Pioneers!*, which Cather referred to as her second first-novel because it was published after *Alexander's Bridge* but was the first to use her native Nebraska materials, her true subject matter.

To break with *McClure's* was not easy, but by 1913 Cather was determined to sink or swim as a professional novelist and never again to commit herself to an employee status if she could possibly avoid it. The intensity of her dedication, the force of her personal determination to put her writing first, last, and always, became legendary. Given the history of her activities in the two decades following university, it is also fully understandable. She was engaged in her quest for perfection; nothing less would satisfy her. And to Cather this endeavor seemed worth whatever sacrifice might be demanded.

New Literary Materials

The years spent in journalism may have been of small literary value to Cather, but a few months spent in the American Southwest provided her with what proved to be indispensable materials. In the spring of 1912, with *Alexander's Bridge* running serially in *McClure's* and publication of "The Bohemian Girl" arranged, Cather traveled by train to Arizona, where her brother Douglass worked for the Santa Fe railroad. The Southwest had always held an attraction for her; its proximity to

Nebraska made the region and its history a part of her general awareness; and even before her first visit to the area, she had written "The
Enchanted Bluff," a story dominated by the image of a southwestern
mesa as a sacred and mysterious goal.

Whereas Cather had reached Europe almost in a spirit of homecom-
ing, of a return to the lands of her forebears and her immigrants, the
American Southwest captured her imagination actively as no other land
had ever captured it. This effect had roots in her childhood feeling that,
in coming to Nebraska, she had wandered perilously close to the edge of
the world; if so, then this was a never-land, beyond the edge. She had
noticed that whenever she was away from the West, she experienced an
appetite to return that manifested itself physically, as a taste in the
mouth, a remembered tang on the tongue. Yet at the same time, Cather
was unable to travel back to the West without a mounting apprehension
of impending loss. Just what she felt doomed to lose she could never say,
but her feeling was similar to that of a nonswimmer who fights the
water irrationally when dropped into it, yet wants to swim. She had the
same urge to struggle whenever she was deposited in the West, and that
emotion served to heighten her awareness and to intensify her sense of
place.[28]

The surface of life in Arizona was not all that attractive. The desert
itself was not so bad—dull red in color and dry, like the dust from
bricks, she thought; unending stretches of rabbitbrush and sage. But
Douglass Cather was headquartered in the town of Winslow, which
impressed his sister as an ugly, desolate little place, with practically nothing to recommend it to a visitor. It was a long, long way from civilization. And its bare grounds were strewn with trash—empty tin cans and
worn-out shoes seemed to predominate—and apparently it was populated entirely by dull railroad people.[29] So far as Willa Cather was concerned, in fact, this isolated desert town had only two redeeming
features. One was a good hotel with a fine restaurant (because the Sante
Fe trains lacked dining cars, Winslow was a handy place to stop and eat),
and the second was its closeness to other localities served by the railroad
(which made it easy to get away when one had had enough). One spot
Cather wanted to visit was New Mexico, and she thought Douglass
might take her to Albuquerque, where she could headquarter while visiting the Indian villages nearby. But Douglass took her instead to
Flagstaff, in northern Arizona. The remains of the aboriginal cliff
dwellings were to be their destination.

It was in Walnut Canyon, not far from Flagstaff, that Cather looked upon Anasazi cliff dwellings for the first time. Nothing in her education had prepared her adequately for the breathtaking revelations that came to her there and that remained with her for the rest of her life. She had heard of the ancient people, of course, but had never before encountered their relics; and the sense of history these abandoned sites stimulated in her had a galvanic effect. In time, this discovery of ancient cultures in America came to be woven into *The Song of the Lark.* Although that novel was yet three years away from publication, the story was already shaping up in Cather's mind.

In 1915 Cather revisited the Southwest, this time with greater calculation aforehand. Her target now was the Mesa Verde of Colorado and its recently excavated Cliff Palace, a 223-room habitation dating from the thirteenth century. With her friend Edith Lewis, with whom she was now living in New York, Cather traveled to Denver, then down a narrow-gauge rail line to Durango, and from there to Mancos, the railroad stop nearest to Mesa Verde. With 20 miles yet to go, the two women located a brother of Richard Wetherill, the cowboy who in 1888 swam the Mancos River on his horse while searching for strayed cattle and found instead the cliff dwellings. In 1915 no automobile road led to Mesa Verde, so a team and driver were hired to make the trip. Although Mesa Verde had been granted national park status in 1906, its isolation discouraged visitors, and so for most of a week Cather and Lewis were the only guests.

So affected was she by this glorious country, Cather wrote Elizabeth Sergeant, that she found it impossible to say anything intelligible except that it drove her crazy with delight. Photographs failed to do it justice; the place was too large, too grand and various. The ruins that appeared on available postcards were no more than samples, she discovered, for similar relics were stuck all around the mesa like the nests of birds—inaccessible, 1,000 feet from the closest vantage point, to be examined only with the aid of binoculars. To Cather, the cliff dwellings meant something very special, and this was what had brought her back to the West. She was not just a curious tourist, and the cliff dwellings were not merely interesting phenomena without much meaning to the modern world. Instead, as David Harrell has pointed out, "she saw them as points along a continuum of creativity in which she herself was a participant."[30]

Cather was to return to the Southwest time and again in years to come, especially to New Mexico, but already she had soaked up experi-

HIGHLAND PARK PUBLIC LIBRARY

ences that would be brought into important use 10 years later, when she published *The Professor's House*. And her encounter with the New Mexican landscape was to prove equally fruitful, for it would lead directly to *Death Comes for the Archbishop*.[31]

Fame

By 1920 Cather had established the first phase of a major career in fiction and was well on her way to becoming famous. Her *O Pioneers!* (1913) had announced the emergence of a "new" Willa Cather, one who had found her literary bearings and capitulated to her natural materials. Literary critics were convinced of her talent by her evocation of the pioneer era in Nebraska. Even more reassuring to her was a general admiration for her manner of rendering character, that mainspring of fiction. In telling the story of Alexandra Bergson and her struggle to succeed as a farmer on the Divide, Cather had told a good story, yet the book achieved "something finer," as the *New York Times* put it, "a direct, human tale of love and struggle and attainment," and the book was powerful without being strained, combining simple treatment with an intense situation. Most reviewers felt that few American novels in recent years had been more impressive.[32]

In 1915 *The Song of the Lark* had appeared, again to critical applause. Cather's concept of struggle and the convincing manner of her heroine's rise to greatness in the world of music made the novel unusual. There had been many stories based upon opera stars, but, unlike so many of them, Cather's story of Thea Kronborg was neither laughable nor artificial. In a leading literary journal, the *Bookman*, Frederick Tabor Cooper saluted the author in these words: "She has created a group of real persons; she takes us into their homes and makes us share in their joys and sorrows, with a quickening sympathy such as we give to our friends in the real world. And that is a gift that is perhaps quite as rare as a genius for plot-building."[33]

Awareness of the Cather presence on the literary scene was general by 1918. Her next novel would clearly be a touchstone, and fortunately *My Ántonia* turned out to be a masterwork that confirmed her promise. No question about it, said H. W. Boynton, "Miss Cather is an accomplished artist." Cather's third strong heroine in three consecutive novels was Ántonia Shimerda, daughter of an unsuccessful Bohemian immigrant to Nebraska, a girl who persisted doggedly in surviving every blow that life could throw against her and eventually reached a sort of triumph of living. "Here at last," announced Randolph Bourne in the *Dial*, "is an American novel, redolent of the Western prairie, that our most irritated and exacting preconceptions can be content with."[34] Practically no dissent from this view was printed.

Every writer who is recognized in his lifetime knows a time when the cheering rings loudest, and for Cather this period arrived with the 1920s. She was referred to now as a novelist—as distinguished from a *woman* novelist—and, as a major voice in current literature, she swiftly built upon her earlier reputation to attract a reading audience that eagerly anticipated each new book and purchased it in large numbers as it appeared. Her novels were now committed to the young firm of Alfred A. Knopf, and he was unstinting in his efforts to boom her work and add to her prestige, opening the decade with a new collection of her stories, *Youth and the Bright Medusa*, and following it in 1922 with *One of Ours*, the story of an idealistic Nebraska boy who volunteers for service in World War I and is killed in France. For the first time, critical opinions concerning Cather's status as a major novelist clashed—and do to this day, concerning *One of Ours*—but the novel was awarded the Pulitzer Prize in 1923.[35]

In 1923 came *A Lost Lady*, for which the immediate reaction was favorable. To those who had been disappointed by *One of Ours*, this new and extremely brief novel seemed a brilliant recovery. In telling the story of Mrs. Forrester, a young Nebraska widow who fails to live up to the ideals established for her in the mind of young Neil Herbert, Cather drew once again on her early memories of Red Cloud society; and *A Lost Lady* remains one of her outstanding contributions. *The Professor's House* (1925) was considerably different, centering upon a male protagonist in the grip of a depressive siege. It was Cather's darkest picture of American life, brightened only by the inclusion of the interpolated section "Tom Outland's Story," based on the discovery of the cliff dwellings at Mesa Verde. At least one major critic pronounced it "Second Best" Cather, but it has managed to gather a corps of recent admirers who find in it a psychological richness surpassing much of Cather's other work. *My Mortal Enemy* (1926) was almost too brief to be seriously considered a novel, and it did little to influence the Cather reputation except perhaps to focus increased attention upon her style—a "cool, firm" method that steadily evoked admiration among both readers and critics. But when *Death Comes for the Archbishop* appeared in 1927, even the tiny group of dissenters from Cather's general chorus of praise agreed as to its stylistic merits, despite some puzzlement over whether the new novel, being constructed as a series of discrete "panels," truly fell within the definition of the novel, strictly interpreted. In *Death Comes for the Archbishop*, Cather made triumphant use of the materials first opened to her in the cliff-dweller territories of Arizona and New Mexico. These were years when Cather almost literally could do no wrong, and the general consensus was that her new book was a masterpiece, an instant classic.[36]

If the 1920s marked the height of acclaim for Cather, the 1930s saw its nadir. She turned 57 as the decade opened, and her writing not only declined in volume but rarely managed to equal her previous high quality. Friendly reviewers—and most in 1931 were solidly in her corner—found themselves uneasily admiring *Shadows on the Rock*, which was published in that year, just as the Great Depression was getting under way. Less kind were the upcoming Marxist critics, for whom the crucial test of a story was the degree to which it involved itself in economic problems and the class struggle—tests in which the new novel, set in eighteenth-century Quebec, could not possibly achieve a passing score. A leading Marxist critic, Granville Hicks, suggested that Cather's status be reappraised, perhaps reduced to that of "minor artist," and he found *Shadows on the Rock* unacceptable, a pure betrayal, in fact, a symptom of "failure of the will."[37]

A new book of stories, *Obscure Destinies* (1932), was considerably closer to vintage Cather and, significantly, marked Cather's last successful effort to mine her early Nebraska memories for fiction. Especially in the story "Neighbour Rosicky," she was successful, and that story in recent years has remained an anthology favorite. *Lucy Gayheart* (1935) and *Sapphira and the Slave Girl* (1940), although much sold and much read, marked an unmistakable decline. When Willa Cather died in New York City on 24 April 1947, among the many honors she had achieved were the Pulitzer Prize, the Prix Femina, and the Gold Medal for fiction awarded by the National Institute of Arts and Letters. But honors such as these are indicative only, and they play less of a role in shaping reputations as time goes on. Now Cather belongs to history; and, as I attempt to demonstrate in a later chapter, "history" currently is bringing in a verdict that is favorable indeed.

Chapter Three
The Early Novels, 1912–1918

My first novel, *Alexander's Bridge*, was very like what painters call a studio picture. . . . Like most young writers, I thought a book should be made out of "interesting materials," and at that time I found the new more exciting than the familiar.

Willa Cather, 1931

Cather's wish to reject outright her first book-length story is unequivocal. Had she possessed the means and the power, she would have bought up all extant copies of *Alexander's Bridge* and seen them destroyed. That ·not being possible, she took every opportunity to disown the book and label it a great mistake. But if it was a mistake, it was one from which, fortunately, she was able to recover.

Alexander's Bridge

The problem with *Alexander's Bridge* is not that it is a bad novel. On the contrary, it is a rather good novel, competent, pleasant, and in fact a nice example of its type, which is the Henry James–inspired exploration of a man's psychological baggage, in this instance the heavy load of regret carried by a builder of bridges whose great example fails because he has knowingly compromised his talent. As her protagonist, Cather elected to center upon a man, one cast in the conventional mold. Bartley Alexander, somewhat as one might imagine his world-conquering namesake, stands tall, six feet of "strength and cordiality and rugged, blond good looks." He is the engineer of all engineers, a man whose photograph exemplifies his profession "because he looked as a tamer of rivers ought to look. Under his tumbled sandy hair his head seemed as hard and powerful as a catapult, and his shoulders looked strong enough in themselves to support a span of any one of his ten great bridges that cut the air above as many rivers."[1]

This superman image is what meets the public gaze and creates the engineer as a world celebrity, but his solid, trustworthy exterior masks a weakness within, a fatal inability always to hold true to the course of his instincts regarding design and building materials. This aspect of Cather's story was given emphasis when *McClure's Magazine* serialized her manuscript under the variant title *Alexander's Masquerade*.

The famous engineer is engaged in his most ambitious and difficult project, a great bridge at Moorlock, in Canada, intended to be the longest cantilever span in existence. But the master builder's style is cramped by niggardly financial backers. With an insufficiency of money to do the job properly, Alexander, instead of refusing to continue with the commission, allows himself to approve the use of lighter structural materials than he knows are required. "The Moorlock bridge," he admits candidly, "is a continual anxiety" to him, being built far too close to the strain limits of the materials. "It's all very well if everything goes well,"[2] he rationalizes. But everything does not go well. The great bridge collapses, plunging Alexander into the wild river below. He perishes, along with some 70 of his workers.

Alexander's Bridge is written in the elegantly spare prose Willa Cather had mastered by this time, and as a story it is nothing to be ashamed of. Its great weakness is its derivative quality, its typicality, the fact that it offers little that is truly unique and might too easily have come from the pen of any of a dozen other competent writers of the day. The fault is not in its method but in its contents. There is almost no spot at which one would be moved to exclaim, as might happen with almost any of her later offerings, "This is a *Willa Cather Novel!*"

Too much of Cather's first novel occurs in London and Boston; too many pages are occupied by a conventional and somewhat pointless romance between the hero and Hilda Burgoyne, a beautiful and successful actress; and everything about the story is turned away, very far away, from Cather's "home pasture"—except for a plaintive image momentarily glimpsed from the window of a speeding train. A group of Canadian boys huddle around a campfire beside a river. Seeing this tableau, Alexander for one nostalgic moment is swept back to his origins and his memory of "a campfire on a sandbar in a Western river." Soul-struck by this strong image, the bridge builder regrets that he can never again go back in time and sit with these carefree boys; "He could remember exactly how the world had looked then."[3]

It is very much as if Cather, well on the way to concluding *Alexander's Bridge*, is impelled to provide her audience with one rapid subliminal flash of the subject matter and locale that she knew she *ought* to be writing about and wished she *were* writing about: the West of her girlhood.

O Pioneers!

In writing her second first-novel, close upon the heels of *Alexander's Bridge*, Willa Cather brushed aside the world and the paraphernalia of Henry James, turning her back upon the Atlantic seaboard and London and the drawing-room company of ladies and gentlemen of polite urban society and instead focused her vision upon the West, the raw Nebraska of the 1880s. Rejecting the linear-plotted, male-centered novel tradition to which she had conformed, Cather now wrote in its place a story composed of discrete scenes widely separated in chronological time and dominated by the first of her strong female protagonists, Alexandra Bergson. *O Pioneers!* marked a glad return to the materials of Cather's Nebraska youth, but with a changed attitude concerning life on the Divide.

It is true that the opening scenes of the novel are grim. They place the reader in the fragile hamlet of Hanover as it desperately attempts to save itself from being "blown away" by a savage and ceaseless winter blast sweeping the frozen prairie. These scenes evoke every bit of that terrifying sense of fear Cather had felt as a child, the apprehension that her family had carried her to a precarious point of no return beyond the edge of the world itself. But soon a new sense of that high tableland known as the Divide emerges and then dominates the novel. Looked at through Alexandra's loving eyes, the land is seen as both friendly and fruitful. The lengthy opening portion of the story concluded, the rest of the novel takes place under clear blue skies during summer seasons; the action occurs chiefly out of doors in the ripe wheat fields and the blossoming orchards. The sole exception here is the coda, whose chilly October weather seems altogether in tune symbolically with the pessimism of its prison setting.

This beneficent portrayal of nature supports and harmonizes with the central figure, Alexandra, a woman for whom Cather solicits the greatest possible admiration. Alexandra represents the best of those pioneers who did *not* fail or lose heart in the face of desperate times. Cather insisted, as her novel took shape, that the land itself was emerging (rightly, she felt) as its "hero," telling this to both Zoe Akins and Elizabeth Sergeant. But the dominating figure is unmistakably Alexandra, with her indomitable "faith in the high land," her unshakable sense of purpose, her clarity of goal, and her willingness to both wait and work for the success that eventually is hers.

O Pioneers! contains a number of subordinate plot lines that serve well to contrast with the central story of Alexandra's struggle and achievement. There are the stories of her brothers Lou and Oscar, for instance, farmers who possess none of their sister's vision, no happy sense of the future, and are men who must come to her bountiful orchard to pick cherries because "they had neither of them had the patience to grow an orchard of their own."[4] Their meager lives are circumscribed by their personal limitations, and their narrowness exhibits itself eventually in pinched features, Lou earning a face that is "thin and shrewd and wrinkled about the eyes, while Oscar's is thick and dull."[5] But their sister grows steadily more attractive and at 40 "seems sunnier and more vigorous than she did as a girl. [She has] the same clear eyes, and she still wears her hair in two braids wound round her head,"[6] braids from which loose ends escape to catch the light and create a sanctifying nimbus in the sunlight.

The obvious danger here of romanticizing Alexandra beyond all credibility is avoided (narrowly) by the power of other contrasting plots and thematic strands. One of these involves Cather's treatment of the corrupting materialism that attacks the children of the pioneers, an acquisitiveness so corrosive that the second generation on the Divide emerges, for the most part, as a lesser breed, whose interests increasingly center upon possessions and status. "We grow hard and heavy here," reflects Alexandra; "our minds get stiff. If the world were no wider than my cornfields, if there was not something besides this [prosperity], I wouldn't feel that it was much worth while to work."[7]

But Lou and Oscar Bergson have far too little imagination to mind a life comprised chiefly of petty and repetitive actions or of flitting from one inconsequential short-term goal to the next. And they are presented as being more typical than not of their generation. The new wealth produced by the land during favorable growing seasons eats like acid through frontier ideals, spreading discontent among the children of the pioneers. A mania for standardization dissipates the strong, unique qualities once found everywhere on the Divide. The linguistic heritage of the original settlers is an early casualty. The Swedish Lou Bergson prides himself on speaking "like anybody from Iowa"—meaning like descendants of the native English speakers who populated that neighboring state. And Lou's wife develops a terror of being "caught" speaking Swedish, even at home. Cather clearly sees this trend as a sad loss of cultural treasures.

The new, lesser feeling invades the homes, whose living rooms attempt to ape the display windows of department stores and whose dining rooms must be stuffed unnecessarily with highly varnished chairs, colored glass, and fussy china sufficient "to satisfy the standards of the new prosperity." This menace to authenticity works pernicious results among the families, including those of the Bergsons. On the threshold of personal happiness—already postponed far too long in favor of duty and her commitment to the land—Alexandra hears her suitor, Carl Linstrum, branded as a fortune hunter by her moneygrubbing brothers. Having conveniently forgotten that when times were hard they had pushed for selling out and retreating to urban factories as hired hands, Lou and Oscar now attempt to forbid Alexandra to place "our property, our homestead" in the hands of a stranger. The spread of dissension among these second-generation Bergsons is one of the saddest pages Willa Cather ever wrote. The idealistic vision of their pioneer father shatters when Alexandra feels obligated to dismiss her unworthy brothers with the advice that if they wish to restrain her from freely disposing of property that is legally hers, they had better consult their lawyers: "And I advise you to do what they tell you; for the authority you exert by law is the only influence you will ever have on me again."[8] Alexandra understands that communication reduced to legal memoranda represents the ultimate deterioration of personal relationships gone bad. "I think," she sighs, "I would rather not have lived to find out what I have today."[9]

The accumulated stress that alienates Alexandra from her brothers is one part of what her success has cost her. "We pay a high rent, though we pay differently," she says, capturing a portion of her philosophy of life. But the greatest payment life exacts is the one that emerges from the major subplot of the novel, concerning the ill-fated romance between Emil Bergson, Alexandra's younger brother, and Marie Shabata. Following their parents' deaths, Alexandra has raised Emil to have a life as different as possible from those of Lou and Oscar. Accomplishing this involves a careful nurturing of Emil's natural talents and includes four years of university education (a "first" for the Bergsons), followed by the broadening experience of residence in Mexico City and plans to study law. But Emil, returning to the Divide at age 21, falls desperately in love with Marie, a Bohemian girl two years his senior and married to Frank Shabata. The Shabata marriage has been a mismatch, and the unhappy Marie reciprocates Emil's feelings for her. One night her extremely jealous and hot-tempered husband discovers the lovers in each other's arms, lying beneath a white mulberry tree at the corner of his orchard, and, having brought his 405 Winchester from the house, he murders them both in a fit of passion.

"Why did it have to be my boy?" is Alexandra's answerless lament, only half aware that she has thought of Emil as considerably more a son than a brother and has lavished on him all of the pent-up maternal care that has had no other outlet. She had been determined that in that world wider than her cornfields, Emil would have his chance, "a whole chance." It would be he who would function as a surrogate to provide the complete meaning of her own long, difficult, and unswerving struggle. That meaning lost with Emil's death, it remains for her to pick up the pieces of her smashed life and struggle forward. And being Alexandra, this, of course, is what she does, eventually reaching something very close to the stoic position, a point of resignation to the forces that have, willy-nilly, shaped her end. She plans to salvage what she can of her emotional self in a passionless marriage with her old friend Carl Linstrum, who, getting news of her tragedy, has come back to Nebraska from his travels. What is salvageable for Alexandra is considerably less than what the joys of love might have been in the warm heyday of youth, but she feels that linking her life now with Carl's will somehow manage to put her "at peace with the world." She feels less happy than content. "I haven't any fears," she confides in her husband-to-be; "I think when friends marry, they are safe. We don't suffer like—those young ones."[10]

The Song of the Lark

Willa Cather's next novel, following closely on the heels of *O Pioneers!*, is her definitive study of the artist and her necessary devotion to her art. *The Song of the Lark*, although drawing heavily upon the life story of Cather's opera-singer friend Olive Fremstad (1871–1951), derived also from the hundreds of reviews of artistic performances Cather had written across the years; came from innumerable interactions with actors, singers, painters, and other writers; and sprang, of course, from her own 40 years of immersion in the artistic struggle. It is no wonder that Cather pronounced this the most interesting of all her novels to write.

Whereas Alexandra Bergson could only dream of a world wider than her cornfields, Cather's new western heroine, Thea Kronborg, ventures forth not only to engage that broader universe but to subdue it. Even the insular subculture of Thea's boondocky hometown, Moonstone, Colorado, is obligated to recognize the glory of the young girl's singing voice, a natural gift apprehended anew by each of her voice coaches. "It all goes back to her original endowment, her tremendous musical talent," explains Thea's midlife fiancé, Fred Ottenburg. Something akin to that sentiment had been expressed also by the eccentric Herr Wunsch, Thea's first musical teacher: "There is only one big thing—desire."[11]

Talent and desire, yes, but more is required—a great deal of hard work. For the road from Moonstone to the stage of the Metropolitan Opera is a long and difficult one. But Thea comes to understand this, to accept it, and willingly to pay the toll, which amounts to no less than the sacrifice of all other phases of her existence. That is the cost of a perfect career. Talent, desire, and persistent effort—the combination of these elements accounts for Thea's success story, which is told in a heavily documented technique in this lengthiest of all Cather novels. It also is her most conventional—as regards form, in particular—as if the story of Thea's struggle and rise in the musical world were of such overriding importance that any experimentation with the manner of telling might amount to a disastrous tampering with perfection. In *The Song of the Lark* Cather appeared to have accepted Emile Zola's advice that life would supply the plot for a story and the writer's duty was to put that story down on paper in all its detail.

Obviously, there is much of Cather herself in the story of Thea Kronborg. More than most artists, perhaps, Cather understood from personal experience the renunciations demanded of her who dared dream of a major career in any of the arts. In many ways *The Song of the Lark* approximates the saga of its author. That was an engrossing story and one that Cather must have been tempted to tell, but fortunately, she did not need to ask Houghton Mifflin to publish a disguised autobiography as her new novel. As luck would have it, she had come upon an achieving woman whose life in some respects paralleled her own: Olive Fremstad, then at the peak of her popularity as a star of the Metropolitan Opera. In 1913, as one of her final responsibilities for *McClure's Magazine*, Cather had interviewed Fremstad and been struck by the manner in which the Swedish-born singer from a small town in frontier Minnesota had emerged on the international scene. She had come, wrote Cather in *McClure's*, "out of a new, crude country, fought her way against every kind of obstacle, and conquered by sheer power of will and character."[12]

That statement by itself might serve as an adequate plot summary of the novel, and Fremstad's career bore an uncanny resemblance to Cather's own experience, a resemblance that could not have been wholly lost on the author. Fremstad, for instance, was just a year older than Cather and had come to the outlands of Minnesota with her (adoptive) parents at the age of six. Her childhood in the small town of St. Peter resembled that lived by Cather in Red Cloud, for both towns were whistlestops that, as Cather described St. Peter, lacked any semblance of artistic stimulus or discriminating taste. To grow up in such an unpromising place was an experience Cather would have had no difficulty at all relating to.

Cather seems to have sensed intuitively and at once that Fremstad must serve as the chief model for the singer in her novel of an "Artist's Youth," as she first thought of entitling her new book. Feeling a personal kinship with her model at so many points in the story, as she apparently did, it seems no wonder that the composition of *The Song of the Lark* should have proceeded rapidly and, in fact, according to Cather, seemed almost to write itself.

The novel focuses upon art; and the principles that it reinforces are the identical principles Cather had observed as she engaged in her own work. They include the belief that one's art is the single thing worth whatever sacrifice may be demanded, as well as a corollary belief that the dedication required of the true artist mandates a good deal of isolation from society and its demands; the necessary consequence is loneliness. Accomplishment in art is very much a solitary quest. The quest is pursued alone, the rewards are enjoyed alone, and the death of both is to be found in those cheap compromises by which an artist might mistakenly attempt to shortcut her path toward absolute perfection.

In depicting Thea's struggle and accomplishment, Cather used much the same principle of contrast with other characters that had served her well in *O Pioneers!* All during her life, Thea Kronborg is surrounded by partial and total failures; and against the deficiencies revealed in other lives, Thea's qualities glow with a special and revealing light. The conditions of life, announces this novel, are secondary to the indispensable determinants such as talent, energy, passion, and dedication. Intelligence is another essential, one of the most important of all. This is a book in which the word *stupid* plays a considerable role, and it invariably serves as a foil for intelligence, as in old Henry Biltmer's observation about the cliff dwellers and their water jugs: "The stupid women carried water for most of their lives; the cleverer ones made the vessels to hold it."[13] A major section of the novel is, in fact, subtitled "Stupid Faces."

The novel is crowded with artists and would-be artists, but none except Thea Kronborg possesses all the traits that combine to make a genuine and top-level success. These traits and their possessor shine all the more brilliantly when juxtaposed against the shortcomings of other, lesser aspirants. There is, for example, Thea's Aunt Tillie, bereft of any natural talent and existing somehow on empty daydreams of accomplishment that serve only to mark her as an eccentric. There is Thea's Moonstone "rival," Lily Fisher, soloist with the local Baptist choir, possessed of a small voice she manages to combine rather cleverly with sentimental song choices and declamatory pieces in order to achieve a local popularity that masks the thinness of her talent. Having reached the outer limits of her ability, Lily cannot go further, as Thea can. Herr Wunsch, who coaches Thea in Moonstone, was once a promising musical artist in his own right, but early on he suffered a fatal loss of nerve; a deficient sense of confidence sapped his stamina, and he has long since capitulated in the struggle for a big career. In Chicago Thea studies voice with Madison Bowers, once a baritone of great promise but held back from a fruitful career by a lack of warmth and enthusiasm, which audiences are quick to detect. They sense the chilliness in his performances, some suggestion of contempt for his listeners, who consequently reject him.

In New York Thea has the example of Madame Necker of the Metropolitan Opera. Necker is a true artist, possessed of the equipment, the desire, and the stamina to reach the top rungs of her profession. But she has not taken proper care of her voice, has adopted a "bad method" that has produced quick results vocally but has also, over the long haul, wrecked her instrument. Thea laments the fact that Necker is "breaking up early," at precisely the moment when she should be singing at her finest. "If she weathers this winter through, it'll be her last,"[14] Thea is convinced. Necker's is the saddest failure of all, but nature is unforgiving of error. And the failures are swept into life's rubbish and discarded, forgotten. They leave no lasting scar and do not affect the future, Thea is told. But Thea herself manages to avoid every temptation, every obstacle; and thereby she establishes herself as the paradigm of the artist.

Does it all proceed too easily, this successful career of Thea's? No, for the road to the top is pitted and strewn with boulders that impede the artist's progress. Jealousies are as inevitable as disappointments. "You get to hating people who do contemptible work and still get on as well as you do," Thea confides to her longtime friend Dr. Archie; "There are many disappointments in my profession, and bitter, bitter contempts."[15] Only one thing seems to remain true: the fact that anything good is going to prove to be expensive. As it had been with Alexandra Bergson, so it is with Thea Kronborg: the price one pays for success is high.

In *The Song of the Lark* Cather made her first major use of the cliff-dweller materials she had come upon in Arizona in 1912. Near the midpoint in her novel, she gave these impressive and, for her, extremely significant ruins a discrete section subtitled "The Ancient People." Here the remains left by the cliff dwellers work the same therapeutic, revelatory effect upon Thea Kronborg that they had worked upon Cather herself. Love, for Thea, has been something of secondary importance through her early youth, pushed out of the way by her concentration on music. But at 19, in Chicago, her career advancing satisfactorily but her spirits flagging nevertheless, she meets Philip Frederick Ottenburg, son of a wealthy St. Louis brewer, who senses that she is stagnating professionally and proposes a change.

Ottenburg's father owns a whole canyon full of cliff-dweller ruins in Arizona near the Navajo reservation, Fred tells Thea, a quiet spot where she can rest at no expense for two or three months. She will come out of the experience "a new girl," Fred Ottenburg assures her—and he is right, for in Panther Canyon Thea gains an entirely fresh lease on life. It comes not only from the great and salutary change away from a crowded, dark, hard-surfaced, and wintry Chicago into forests of fresh pine, sparkling mountain air, and snowy summits. All of these work on her for the better psychologically, as she had expected they might, being so close to "the earliest sources of gladness that she could remember."[16] The surprise is her personal discovery of the cliff dwellers' remains, not merely their cleverly designed stone dwellings strategically placed like nests in clefts of the rock canyon, but more particularly the amazingly decorated potsherds that seem to be scattered everywhere in the relatively untouched site. Her imagination working actively on these fragments of artistic effort from the past, Thea comes to understand that ages ago Indian women had lavished all their energies on making—without the help of a potter's wheel—lovely artifacts "to house the precious water" around which all their tribal customs and ceremonies and religion revolved: "Their pottery was their most direct appeal to water, the envelope and the sheath of the precious element itself."[17]

Dwelling on these ancient endeavors, Thea begins to feel a deep kinship with the ancient people, a link with them established by a commonality she realizes is Art. This epiphany comes to her one morning as she stands in a sunny pool at the floor of the canyon, bathing in that same water so treasured by the Indian women:

> The stream and the broken pottery: what was any art but an effort to make a sheath, a mould in which to imprison for a moment the shining, elusive element which is life itself—life hurrying past us and running away, too strong to stop, too sweet to lose? The Indian women had held

it in their jars. . . . In singing, one made a vessel of one's throat and nostrils and held it on one's breath, caught the stream in a scale of natural intervals. . . . Not only did the world seem older and richer to Thea now, but she herself seemed older. . . . Her ideas were simplified, became sharper and cleaner. She felt united and strong.[18]

Her depression beaten now by the encounter and the revelation, her spirit restored, Thea feels ready to return to the East and to resume her career.

Thea does achieve what she has worked for, so long, so patiently—stardom at the Metropolitan Opera in Wagnerian roles. One afternoon, well into her career, she at last feels that she has come into "full possession of things she had been refining and perfecting for so long. . . . All that deep-rooted vitality flowered in her voice, her face, in her very finger-tips. She felt like a tree bursting into bloom."[19] Now Thea has proven to be a true artist, has proven this to her severest critic: herself. And that is the point toward which *The Song of the Lark* has been heading all along, that truth concerning art, that one participates in it finally to earn one's own approval. Nothing else matters very much, neither the struggle nor the renunciation. The world may take its pound of flesh, but time cannot erase one's triumphant self-knowledge of genuine accomplishment.

My Ántonia

In 1919, for the third time in a five-year span, Cather published a novel glorifying a woman's strength. It may well be her masterpiece. Critical opinions may vary somewhat here, but there are no Cather scholars I know of who would not insist that *My Ántonia* be placed close to the top of any list of her indispensable works.

Very unlike either *O Pioneers!* or *The Song of the Lark*, this new novel does not concern success achieved via conventionally understood routes or represented by conventional markers (large holdings of valuable land; a well-paying artistic career). The heroine, Ántonia Shimerda, has in fact almost nothing that might serve to set her apart automatically from the common herd, to mark her, as it were, as a person to watch. Alexandra and Thea from their beginnings are extraordinary; Ántonia is ordinariness personified. Or so she seems, on the surface of things. It is the triumph of Cather's rapidly advancing skill as a writer that in *My Ántonia* the alchemy of her art transforms apparent dross into spun gold.

To summarize the plot of this novel is to demonstrate its common threads. An immigrant Bohemian girl, the daughter of a suicide, is trapped in the drabbest possible conditions on the Nebraska Divide, then is indentured to an unappreciative town family as a hired girl. She is uneducated, lacking in any special talents, so naive as to be easy prey to the first glib scoundrel who sets his eye upon her. Eventually she becomes the wife of a not-overly-achieving farmer and in true obscurity raises a sizable family. Yet out of this seemingly unpromising material Cather created a classic, and Ántonia's is that rarest of Cather's lives—a joyous one.

The girl's great quality is a natural zest for life that sends her always plunging into the mainstream of local activity, disregardful of money, status, possessions, or career (it might, in fact, be questioned whether Ántonia has any realistic knowledge of such worldly things). She appears to live merely for the rich experience of living itself, but she does this with such a sense of the indomitable that her existence matches or surpasses both Alexandra's rage for farming and Thea's dedication to her voice. Probably because Ántonia has not set great store on "winning," she is not destroyed by "losing"; she emerges relatively unscathed from ordeals that might ruin a lesser spirit. Her "talents" include the gift of a warm heart, a buoyant sense of humor, and an infinite capacity for enthusiasm. These are not small gifts.

The life lived by Ántonia (who, as noted earlier, is based upon a Bohemian hired girl the author knew as a child in Red Cloud) was as foreign to Cather as firmament to fin, and in that difference may lie the secret of her appeal as a subject for fiction. The Theas and the Alexandras of the world Cather knew well and understood intimately, for in so many ways they stood as surrogates for her own hungering after worldly achievement and public acclaim. She could analyze such women without difficulty and lay out their salient traits for readers in a good, lucid story. But Ántonia defied the ordinary process of analysis, requiring not understanding so much as worship. She was to be marveled at, something like a phenomenal natural object—a sequoia perhaps—that looms up in front of the viewer as a living contradiction of everything he has ever thought he understood about trees.

Something of this sort may be what Cather had in mind when she told Elizabeth Sergeant that she wanted her portrait of Ántonia to resemble a pot of lovely flowers set all by itself in the center of a table, on display, a rare object "which one may examine from all sides. I want her to stand out—like this—because she *is* the story."[20] Such a desire, that Ántonia should be seen from a variety of angles, may account for the narrative device Cather adopted especially for the novel. This time, rather than using herself—the author—as a means of establishing the viewpoint, Cather employed a specific narrator, a man. The use of the male persona allowed her to objectify the portrait, necessary because of her own emotional closeness to the model, and to deal with the sexual aspects of Ántonia's life from a more readily understandable, more plausible position and one that would serve to enrich the story thematically. Surely the invented, male Jim Burden is freer than Cather would be to feel romantically drawn to Ántonia and to express the emotional effects of the sexual tug. Also, because Jim is the product of a repressed and biased society, he serves at the same moment to dramatize the gulf separating the socially "in" group of Black Hawk (the Anglo-Saxons) from the "out" group (the mid-European immigrants). Questions regarding social power, exclusion, and alienation could be entertained through the figure of Jim, who wishes to be a suitor for Ántonia's hand but dares not buck the existing mores of his place and time. One senses that Jim regrets passing up his opportunity, regrets it bitterly, and also that his present involvement in an unhappy marriage gives that regret an especially ironic tinge; and all of these feelings help to explain and authenticate Jim's deeply nostalgic view of the woman who, but for his own regrettable weaknesses, might have become Mrs. James Burden and made him a happier man.

It seems quite plausible that Cather, coming to understand full well the toll exacted on one's privacy by a public career (so heavily thematic in the stories of Alexandra and Thea) came also to admire—even to envy—lives lived in such obscurity and so casually as Ántonia's. Her use of Jim Burden as narrator verifies the structure of the novel, a series of discrete "panels" whose time, place, and action are determined by the manner in which Jim's memories happen to arise, roughly chronological but with considerable leaps in time occurring between the individual panels. As readers, we do see Ántonia from various "sides"—the differing angles at which her life's path has crossed that of Jim Burden: as a child, as an adolescent, as a maiden in lovely bloom, as a mature and experienced woman, and finally as a wife and mother. Because the narrator himself grows older as the story progresses, and because his own experiences alter his life and personality, each successive side from which Ántonia is viewed becomes more complex and, indeed, more interesting. That complexity is increased by the fact that Jim at times sees Ántonia not directly but at second hand, through the eyes of others. Ultimately,

Cather's choice of narrative devices explains and determines the title of the novel, for the manuscript that ostensibly forms the greater share of the book is, as Jim Burden himself puts it, the story of *my* Ántonia and no one else's.

Ántonia surpasses previous Cather heroines in maintaining an integrated personality, is able to avoid both Thea Kronberg's rather dry (and increasingly so) preoccupation with herself and her music and Alexandra Bergson's sense of confinement and alienation, the sad conviction that somehow her success at farming the Divide has cost her too high a price. By way of contrast, then, Ántonia in her middle years, though the survivor in a life that has been rough indeed, seems to Jim to shine "in the full vigor of her personality, battered but not diminished." Cather is explicit in establishing the point that Ántonia at heart remains as life loving as when she first rode the Burlington train into the Nebraska Divide. Her great secret is that of enthusiasm, her retention of a sheer childlike delight in existence itself, a zest for life that is missing in Jim Burden's wife, for instance, a woman "temperamentally incapable of enthusiasm,"[21] a quality that somehow has been lost along the way by Jim.

Ántonia Shimerda, with all of life's disadvantages arranged against her, somehow by force of spirit transcends every life blow and does so seemingly without soiling herself. That Cather was able to capture the essence of such a personality without allowing the portrait—and the novel—to mire down in a romantic quicksand is the chief magic worked here by Cather, who displays her virtuosity as a consummate artist. The novel builds to a crescendo of praise for the immigrant Bohemian girl who never left Nebraska but somehow managed to travel further—higher—in life than any of the more favored few of Black Hawk. We do not blanch from the paean that closes *My Ántonia* because, having been well prepared for it, we agree that the eulogy has been earned:

> She lent herself to immemorial human attitudes which we recognize by instinct as universal and true. She was a battered woman now, not a lovely girl, but she still had that something which fires the imagination, could still stop one's breath for a moment by a look or gesture that somehow revealed the meaning in common things. She had only to stand in the orchard, to put her hand on a little crab tree and look up at the apples, to make you feel the goodness of planting and tending and harvesting at last. All the strong things of her heart came out in her body, that had been so tireless in serving generous emotions.
>
> It was no wonder that her sons stood tall and straight. She was a rich mine of life, like the founders of early races.[22]

Chapter Four
Novels of the Middle Years, 1922–1927

Who, when *A Lost Lady* was her latest work, could have foreseen *The Professor's House*, or who, reading that in 1925, could have guessed that it would be followed in quick succession by books as different from each other as *My Mortal Enemy* and *Death Comes for the Archbishop*?

René Rapin, 1930

During the 1920s, Cather published five novels in rapid succession, all of them coming out during the five years between 1922 and 1927. For Cather these were years of furious concentration on her rapidly expanding career, years of nonstop writing. They were times also of accelerating critical acclaim, times when her popularity with readers made huge gains. By 1918 and the publication of *My Ántonia*, Cather was "noticed" and her promise recorded; by 1927 her name had become something of a household word, and *Death Comes for the Archbishop* was being proclaimed a masterwork. The remarkable productivity of these middle years (Cather had entered her fifties) was uneven, involving some of the author's slightest works of fiction as well as some of her most enduring titles. But, taken altogether, the 1920s saw Willa Cather solidly established among the most prominent authors in America.

One of Ours

One sign of Cather's prominence on the literary landscape came with the awarding of the Pulitzer Prize in fiction to her novel *One of Ours* in 1923. The novel is not one of her best, and it evoked no end of critical controversy—even scorn—upon its publication in 1922. But the author's fame had been growing rapidly, based largely upon the enduring popularity of *O Pioneers!*, *The Song of the Lark*, and *My Ántonia*, and it was helped along by a brilliant collection of stories, *Youth and the Bright Medusa*, published in 1920. It was not the first time in the brief history of the Pulitzer Prize that the laurels were placed upon a writer's second-best work, nor would it be the last.

47

Cather's subject in *One of Ours* was World War I and the death in battle of "one of our own" American soldiers who had sailed for France to
make the world safe for democracy. Therein lay the basis for much of the
folderol, all of which inquired in one way or another as to whether, war
being regarded as something of a male province, a woman with no direct
experience of war could—or should—undertake such a project. "Poor
woman, she had to get her war experience somewhere," and so she
cribbed it from the works of other writers; so said young Ernest
Hemingway in *The Torrents of Spring* (1926). The remark was not untyp-
ical. An immediate stimulus for *One of Ours* was the death in France of
Private G. P. Cather, Willa's 35-year-old cousin from Bladen, Nebraska,
who was killed in battle and whose body was brought back to Nebraska
for burial in 1921. The Great War, as it was then called, was a traumat-
ic event for every mature citizen of Western civilization, but more especially, perhaps, for those in the arts, whose task it is to react to events
and to record impressions, effects, and interpretations. These reactions
do not always occur immediately; an extensive period of time may elapse
between an event such as a war and the artistic statement of its impact.
In Cather's case, that pause seems to have lasted for the better part of
four years, and it may not be far off the mark to suggest that the war
was responsible for the unusual hiatus (1918–22) in her production of
novels. *One of Ours*, in fact, appeared almost simultaneously with T. S.
Eliot's *The Waste Land*, which conveyed to the public (at least to its intellectual segment) Eliot's own artistic summation of the societal havoc
wreaked by the conflict.

If Cather realized the problems to be encountered upon tackling a
novel that would concern a war in which she had been no more than a
distant bystander, she could be comforted by the knowledge that for
more than half of her book, which turned out to be rather extensive (459
pages in print), she would be dealing with the people and the farmlands
of Nebraska, home territory. With such materials she always felt secure
of her ground. Whatever the motivation for this long foreground, it had
the result of splitting the novel down the middle thematically, with a
first half devoted to portraying the materialistic cancer as it encroaches
upon American midwestern life, and a second half given over to the tale
of Claude Wheeler's wartime death.

Claude is central to the entire novel (and Cather had wanted to call it
simply *Claude*), but the insurmountable difficulty for her story is that she
elected to place an ineffectual hero in a position where what were needed
were great determination and strength of spirit—precisely the qualities

that shone so brightly in Alexandra, Thea, and Ántonia. By contrast, Claude Wheeler is a young man of uncertain abilities, and while he does have dreams of accomplishment, he possesses no passionate reason for existing. Lacking goals and direction, Claude has no worthwhile target toward which to direct his considerable young male energy: "the old belief flashed up in him with an intense kind of hope, an intense kind of pain—the conviction that there was something splendid about life, if only he could but find it."[1] With this revelation, a gulf opens between Claude Wheeler and Cather's strong heroines, especially those young movers and shakers Alexandra and Thea, who seem from their earliest years to be guided almost genetically toward meaningful goals that stand out like pole stars to urge them on. Like Willa Cather herself, these were women who knew precisely where they wanted to go.

But Claude flounders, the least effectual—the least interesting, unfortunately—of the several characters who dramatize Cather's theme of a society in the process of shedding its great qualities—idealism and the will to struggle—in favor of a fondness for money and whatever money will buy, especially the mechanical products of the industrial era then arriving in full force in America. Cather by 1920–21 had come to see a distinct weakening of the American faith in personal achievement and the consequent replacement of individualism by a new and lesser god, that of standardization (the secret of successful mass production). As a result, Cather's writing of the early 1920s is flooded with a sense of loss, an emotional darkness that bordered upon depression, most directly voiced in her essay "Nebraska: The End of the First Cycle," published contemporaneously with *One of Ours*, which is its fictional counterpart. The essay stands as an elegy for a world lost—a glorious West founded upon the bedrock of indomitable character. "The splendid story of the pioneers is lost," announces Cather. In its place comes only a sorry tale of "pale proprieties [and] the insincere, conventional optimism of our art and thought." Her beloved West was stamped cruelly with an "ugly crest of materialism" whose manifestations were everywhere to be observed:

> Too much prosperity, too many moving-picture shows, too much gaudy fiction have colored the taste and manners of so many of these Nebraskans of the future. There, as elsewhere, one finds the frenzy to be showy: farmer boys who wish to be spenders before they are earners, girls who try to look like heroines of the cinema screen. . . . The generation now in the driver's seat hates to make anything, wants to live and die in

an automobile, scudding past those acres where the old men used to fol-
low the long corn-rows up and down. They want to buy everything
ready-made: clothes, food, education, music, pleasure.[2]

The sad, elegiac tone of Cather's "Nebraska" is the dominant tone also of
One of Ours. The novel expands upon the theme previously touched upon
in *O Pioneers!*, particularly in the characters of Lou and Oscar Bergson,
Nebraskans ruined by the easy life, spoiled by the riches their wild land
has produced, men whose motto is "off with the old, on with the new"
and who feel less comfortable tilling fields than suing their friends and
neighbors in county courtrooms.

The Wheeler family is presented to the reader as a typical case of
Nebraskans caught up in the new spirit. In their farm home on Lovely
Creek, life is changing fast. Mrs. Wheeler and Mahailey—older and part
of the passing scene—cling to what little they can out of an idealism
that really is not much more than a memory. Claude is the sole member
of the younger generation who shares their values—and thereby he is
identified early on with a lost cause. His brothers, Bayliss and Ralph,
along with their father, are in a rush to embrace the new pragmatic
ways. So the Wheelers are offered to the reader as a microcosm in which
the clash of natural goals comes to the fore, and the individual members
of the family are known chiefly by their espousal of the old (good) or of
the new (bad) values that characterize society at large.

Mr. Wheeler is callous and unthinking most of the time, and when he
does express serious concerns they are limited to plans for more land and
larger crops, for sharp dealing with his neighbors, and for speculating as
to how high the war in far-off Europe might drive the price of a bushel
of midwestern wheat. Bayliss Wheeler operates an implement store in
nearby Hanover, drives a new Cadillac, and has as his guiding maxim
the firm belief that everything has its price. Ralph remains on the farm,
but he succumbs in the grand manner to the national mania for machinery for both farm and home. The patent flatirons, oil stoves, mechanical
dishwashers, and other such paraphernalia he lugs back from Hanover
drive Mahailey and Mrs. Wheeler wild. Values are distorted: Mr.
Wheeler gladly pays any inflated price for a new thresher but balks at
buying a cheap meal at the local hotel dining room.

As for Claude, he seems to represent Cather's sad bewilderment with
a society that tells people to consider themselves odd if they try to
explain themselves logically, if they dress with care and taste, or if they
are caught taking pains in any concern. Scene follows scene during this

first half of the story, all showing Claude involved in losing battles. As Cather's mouthpiece, he questions the value of working to accumulate money when it brings nothing one really wants.

Claude's brief stay at the University of Nebraska has opened his eyes to a life in which cash and machinery might find their proper places. The Erlich family, who befriend him, seem to know how to live rightly, spending as little money as possible on machines to do their work or to entertain them. Whatever else machines can do, Claude decides, they can never fabricate pleasure or construct people with agreeable personalities. The things in which the Erlichs indulge—music, books, intelligent conversation, manners, art—seem to Claude to be just the things that truly do lend beauty to life. In the tension between the contrasting lives led by the Wheelers and the Erlichs, the Erlichs are easy victors. But Claude is soon removed from the university atmosphere by his family and returned to the stuffy environment on Lovely Creek (a name which by this time is loaded with ironic overtones).

Perhaps Willa Cather saw her extensive development of the materialism theme, and its crushing effect upon Claude, as marking a parallel with Claude's personal defeat (death) in France, his steady losses against the Wheelers as forecasting his greater loss in the war. Whatever the case, World War I becomes the occasion of Claude's final victimization. In a somewhat golden haze, he envisions the war as a great crusade; that it might prove to be counterfeit has no place in his thinking. As a student of history, his interest has centered upon Joan of Arc, whose single-handed defiance of her opponents despite overwhelming odds seems like a miracle to him, one that makes all things possible. So when war comes, his eagerness to enlist is linked irretrievably with the land in which St. Joan waged her own holy war. To rescue France is the immediate goal of his own personal crusade.

"I never knew," reflects Claude shortly before his death by German fire, "there was anything worth living for till this war came along. Before that the world seemed like a business proposition."[3]

By this time Claude has seen any number of battlefields and shattered villages but none as ugly as he envisions the whole world would become if the Bayliss Wheelers were to control it wholly—and until the war broke out and changed this thinking, he had almost come to believe that the Baylisses *did* control all things. What the war proves to Claude is that the world is safe from cunning and prudence. Claude dies with this illusion intact. That his illusion was not Cather's own is demonstrated perhaps by the final pages of the novel, wherein Claude's mother reluctantly offers thanks that her son died in France because she understands that he was not strong enough to survive the psychic shock of "that last, desolating disappointment" of seeing society's eager return to meanness and greed, of coming to know that the war had been little more than a temporary interruption of sad, sad trends. "He died believing his own country better than it is," reflects Mrs. Wheeler, "and France better than any country can ever be. And these were beautiful beliefs to die with."[4]

One of Ours is an angry novel and a bitter one. And that can be attributed less to the influence on the author of the wasted life of her idealistic soldier cousin than to Cather's own implicit acknowledgment that the holy war for America's soul had foundered.

A Lost Lady

If Cather placed her critical reputation in jeopardy with *One of Ours*, she retrieved it brilliantly with that novel's immediate successor, *A Lost Lady* (1923), which holds up admirably as one of Cather's finest accomplishments. A good deal of the tension between old and new ways, felt so heavily in *One of Ours*, informs this story as well, but in a much quieter manner. Those bitter feelings Cather harbored against the undesirable changes life was bringing—and against those who were the agents of change—are here kept under much tighter control. There is considerably less preaching; rather, the social ideas that motivate the novel are now reined in and made secondary to the characters who represent them and who, rightly, dominate the action.

A Lost Lady recounts the story of Marian Forrester, the youthful and vigorous wife of Captain Daniel Forrester and the most prominent hostess in Sweet Water, Nebraska, the nom de plume here given Red Cloud. The central action is called up from "thirty or forty years ago"—which would place it during the 1880s, the decade of Cather's growing up. The story relies on Cather's memories of Lyra Garber, the wife of Silas Garber, a former railroad baron and ex-governor of the state. Garber had been one of the founders of Red Cloud, and after his gubernatorial term in Lincoln he returned to the town with the young wife he had met in California.

On a knoll just beyond the boundaries of Red Cloud, these two had lived out his retirement in a simple but overly gingerbreaded frame house undistinguished except for the extraordinary quality of the hospitality extended within its walls. It was a house, as Cather puts it in *A Lost Lady*, "well known from Omaha to Denver for its hospitality and for a certain charm of atmosphere."[5]   The governor's health had been impaired by a carriage accident, but whenever it was possible—and when the two were not traveling—the Garbers welcomed visitors. These ordinarily were "important" people, VIPs of the Burlington Railroad and their families who frequently passed through town. But certain citizens of Red Cloud were welcome as well, among them the young Willa Cather. She remembered Lyra Garber as "a flash of brightness in a grey background," and the story of Lyra's romance with the governor, so distant from anything Cather herself was ever to experience in her personal life, both enchanted and mystified her. Decades later, out of these fond but not really very extensive memories, and out of her heartsick impressions of Western decline, Cather fashioned the novella *A Lost Lady*.

In telling her story, Cather worked a variation on the narrative device she had experimented with in *My Ántonia*, so that portions of the story are narrated by herself as the omniscient author, while other—major— portions of the action are filtered through the viewpoint of a townsboy, Niel Herbert. His sporadic yet fairly regular encounters with Marian Forrester are recorded from the time he is 12 until he is middle-aged— somewhere in his forties—but the principal action is over by the time Niel is about 21 and leaving Sweet Water for the last time, to complete his studies at the Massachusetts Institute of Technology.

A Lost Lady concerns that period of history when the original mid- western frontier generation yields to the second and, in Cather's opinion, considerably lesser one. Society is in upheaval. Sunset is falling on the splendid age of the pioneers, a new day dawning on a world less noble, crasser by far, than that golden, Camelot-like moment best represented by the generous exploits of Silas Garber. As Garber's fictional counter- part, Captain Forrester is a man of action, the first and last of the real constructive personalities who built the West and imbued it with their own strong and impeccable sense of ethics. Handsome, capable, cul- tured, become wealthy through his own honest entrepreneurial efforts, and possessed of unimpeachable integrity, Forrester is idealized by Cather as a pillar of Western society.

In opposition to the Captain is Ivy Peters, who stands as representa- tive of that corrupted generation Cather saw as trailing a downward path from the high noon of the homesteaders and railroad builders. He is Lou and Oscar Bergson written large, Bayliss and Frank Wheeler pressed to the nth degree. Ivy, as ugly as he is crafty, as uncouth as grasping, lacks any sense of fair play. For him the West exists not to build upon but to exploit. A pair of contrasting actions clarify the distinctions between Forrester and Peters. The Captain sacrifices his personal fortune in order to protect small depositors in a wrecked bank that is only tangentially linked to his name; Ivy Peters slits the eyes of an innocent woodpecker and looses it back to a world forever darkened. By their deeds shall you know them!

The question of the Forrester marshlands (never drained by the Captain, who loves the region for its intrinsic beauties) furnishes Cather with a major symbol with which to dramatize what she saw as the depredation of the West. Ivy Peters covets the Forrester swamp specifically in order to drain it and raise profitable crops of wheat. When at last he does gain control over the Forrester property, the despoiling of these pleasant but hitherto-unexploited acres serves as an occasion for Cather to make explicit her theme of the West in passage from caring to cynical hands:

> The Old West had been settled by dreamers, great-hearted adventurers who were unpractical to the point of magnificence; a courteous brotherhood, strong in attack, but weak in defense, who could conquer but not hold. Now all the vast territory they had won was to be at the mercy of men like Ivy Peters, who had never dared anything, never risked anything. . . . All the way from the Missouri to the mountains this generation of shrewd young men, trained to petty economies by hard times, would do exactly what Ivy had done when he drained the Forrester marsh.[6]

The beautiful yields to the utilitarian. And Marian Forrester herself, the most purely beautiful object of desire in the story, is likewise possessed and degraded—in Niel's eyes—by Ivy Peters. Clearly these two, the marsh and Marian, represent the same thing: the glorious West of Cather's girlhood. Both are recalled with deep emotion and imbued with the nimbus of nostalgic vision. Marian and the marsh: both had flourished under the appreciative care of the Forrester generation, and both are to suffer grievously from the depredations of the Peters generation.

Marian Forrester is identified by Cather (and through her by Niel Herbert) with all things lovely and fragile. She is highly dependent upon good caretakers. Captain Forrester is precisely this, of course, and so Marian blossoms under his thoughtful ministrations. But these can last only so long as he endures. Unfortunately, the Captain suffers from a disabling accident and then from financial failure. Hard times arrive, the decline of the railroad era is under way, the Captain's infirmity increases, and eventually he passes from the scene, as his era has already passed.

Without his patient guidance, Marian is "like a ship without ballast, driven hither and thither by every wind."[7]

Niel Herbert, Cather's somewhat obtuse narrator, never quite comprehends what the author-as-narrator seems to perceive so clearly: that conditions inevitably change with time, and that people alter along with conditions. The well-meaning but inexperienced and, in fact, callow Niel believes that Mrs. Forrester should have perished with her husband and his era, in something like an act of Indian suttee, perhaps. But Marian is younger than her husband by some 25 years and, barring an act of immolation, is doomed to go on living for some time to come, obliged to accommodate herself to change.

To Niel, Marian appears to be much too concerned with her individual survival on *any* terms. And Marian's matter-of-fact dedication to money, emblem of her survival, is revolting to the overly fastidious Niel. That she can say to him, "Money is a very important thing. Realize that in the beginning, face it, and don't be ridiculous in the end, like so many of us,"[8] is to announce her own demise as an icon of the older, better way. And when Niel then happens to witness Marian's acquiescence when Ivy Peters so nonchalantly comes up behind her in her kitchen, putting his arms about her, "his hands meeting over her breast," Niel is forced to face the extremely painful truth that his glorification of Marian Forrester had been illusory. "All those years he had thought it was Mrs. Forrester who made that house so different from any other,"[9] but it had been the Captain, really. Unable to reconcile himself to the reality, Niel does what young idealists so often do, mistakenly: he disowns the former object of his worship. Rationalizing that he had "given her a year of his life, and she had thrown it away [he told himself that] nothing she could ever do would in the least matter to him again."[10]

But of course it does matter, will always matter. Just as Cather was herself convinced that her West had been cheapened, even demolished, and yet she never could wash her hands of it and feel at peace elsewhere, so Niel Herbert goes on thinking about, and sometimes receiving reports about, Marian Forrester, his beloved, his lost lady. "She hadn't changed as much as you'd think," says Ed Elliot, bringing Niel belated news of his encounter with Marian after her remarriage to a wealthy Argentinean; "She was a good deal made up, of course . . . plenty of powder, and a little red, too, I guess. Her hair was black, blacker than I remembered it; looked as if she dyed it."[11]

By the time he receives this bit of news about the old beauty and her sad efforts to prolong youth, Niel Herbert himself has grown considerably older, is definitely into middle age, and has gained experience into the inevitable changes worked by time. And so the intractable attitude he had adopted in youth has softened. Learning that Marian had never given up on him, much as he might have given up on her, Niel relents, speculating about the possibility of taking an impulsive cruise to Argentina to mend his fences with her. But attorney Niel is anything but impulsive, and he has relented too late. Marian has been dead for three years.

The Professor's House

Ever since *O Pioneers!*, Cather had used her novels as a means of railing against what she saw as the capitulation of twentieth-century Americans to the acquisitive spirit of the times. As money and material objects assumed an increasingly central position in society, idealism gave ground to pragmatism, beauty to practicality. *The Professor's House* (1925) contains Cather's fullest expression of dismay at the directions being taken. In her previous novels that theme had been incidental or at best secondary, but in *The Professor's House* it becomes primary.

To represent her attitudes, Cather employs a male viewpoint, that of Godfrey St. Peter, professor of history at Hamilton University on the shores of Lake Michigan. Dedicated to quality and to the transmission of knowledge, St. Peter has labored for 15 years on his multivolume lifework *Spanish Adventurers in North America*, which has brought him the Oxford Prize of $20,000. With that bonanza, but chiefly to please his wife, St. Peter has built himself a new house.

At middle age, standing at a crossroads in his life, the Professor faces alternatives that are summed up by the contrasts between his two houses. In his old dwelling he has managed to shape his monumental scholarly work without, as Cather puts it, the aid of "filing-cabinets or money or a decent study or a decent stove—and without encouragement, Heaven knew!"[12] But he has known security there, his walled-in garden has been a delight to him, and his barren attic study has been a peaceful retreat from the distractions of the world. His new house, on the point of standing ready for occupancy, is comfortable, grand, and showy. St. Peter cannot help feeling uneasy about relinquishing the old for the new. Until now he has managed to resist the crassness that seems to pervade the modern world, but the ostentation of his new house seems a major concession.

The St. Peter family is split on the issue of this new house. For Mrs. St. Peter it represents an opportunity to shed her former life, which has not been wholly satisfying, and to acquire, along with her new address, the new clothes, new furnishings, new machines, and even new friends that upward mobility seems to demand. St. Peter resists the move, feeling guilt at having allowed himself to consent to the new house but powerless now to prevent the move. He feels deeply the imminent loss of much that he holds dear. The family is divided also on the issue of a revolutionary vacuum tube invented by the Professor's one-time student and protégé Tom Outland. Killed in World War I, Outland had willed his inventor's rights to St. Peter's daughter Rosamond, believing himself to be in love with her. The invention is now being exploited commercially, and Rosamond and her husband, Louis Marsellus, are rapidly becoming rich on profits. But the money—as so often in Cather's stories—is shattering old family harmonies. Particularly affected by the new wealth is St. Peter's other daughter, Kathleen, who does not share in the royalties from the Outland tube and consequently sees herself and Rosamond positioned in different and widely separated socioeconomic castes.

Because the Professor has been adamant in refusing to profit from Outland's invention, he is particularly rankled in watching from the sidelines as the Marselluses live ever more extravagantly. Also, a Mrs. Crane, widow of another professor with whom Outland had worked at Hamilton, is ready to institute a bitter court battle for a share of the royalties, being convinced that her husband's contributions to Outland's ideas entitle her to participate in whatever money the invention is producing. The commercial use of the Outland tube, so beneficial to society, is working havoc among the St. Peterses and among the university faculty. Thinking of this irony, the Professor questions, "Was it for this the light in Outland's laboratory used to burn so far into the night!" and he laments, "If Outland were here tonight he might say with Mark Antony, *My fortunes have corrupted honest men.*"[13]

Indeed, the corruption of otherwise honest men is the principal theme of the novel. And in order to highlight it, but on another plane, Cather took the bold step of breaking her otherwise chronological story open and inserting, just past midpoint, a digression of 74 pages entitled "Tom Outland's Story." Outland's tale is presented as a monologue delivered during a rainy-night colloquy between him and St. Peter on a summer evening when the other family members are vacationing in Colorado. It is based upon Cather's 1915 trip with Edith Lewis to Mesa Verde and in fact stands as her most substantial fictional use of that experience. And Outland's story has nothing at all to do with the chronology of St. Peter's own story except that its theme of defeat tallies with the defeat the Professor is currently sensing, provoked by the trauma of abandoning his old home for the new house. That is an important connection, of course. Tom Outland tells of his youth as a Colorado cowboy exploring the tantalizing Blue Mesa, which juts 1,000 feet from the plain, and of his discovery there of the long-abandoned cliff city, intact, just as though its people one day had quietly, methodically packed up and departed. But even when long emptied of their population, the cliff dwellings persist in speaking of balance and unity, of a reassuring sense of order much at odds with the modern tempo, of a powerful symmetry that is pleasing from any aspect. The harmony of the cliff-dwelling architecture speaks of a community at peace with itself. Something of "the calmness of eternity" pervades the site, convincing Outland that the inhabitants must necessarily have been a fine people.

In every sense, the civilization of the Blue Mesa stands in bold contrast to the modern era that is so stultifying to the Professor. Its people had concentrated upon the arts of peace, not warfare, and they had lived for something considerably more than mere food and shelter. On the Blue Mesa, that truth was everywhere to be seen, but one observed it particularly in the superior shapes and decorative surfaces of the Anasazi water jugs. Guided by Father Duchene of the local Catholic mission, Outland comes to perceive the cliff dwellers as altogether a superior group, and Father Duchene clothes Outland's thoughts in words:

> "I see them here, isolated, cut off from other tribes, working out their destiny, making their mesa more and more worthy to be a home for man, purifying life by religious ceremonies and observances. . . . Like you, I feel a reverence for this place. Wherever humanity has made that hardest of all starts and lifted itself out of mere brutality, is a sacred spot. Your people were cut off here without the influence of example or emulation, with no incentive but some natural yearning for order and security. They built themselves into this mesa and humanized it."[14]

But the ancient people did not prevail against whatever conditions or exigencies caused their sudden removal from the Blue Mesa, and the relics they left behind them do not prevail against the wanton practices of the modern age, either. Hoping to preserve his marvelous find, his treasure trove of Anasazi artifacts, Outland travels to Washington, where he comes to realize that no one has any genuine interest in it. One official "borrows" some choice specimens from the examples Outland has brought with him, and Outland understands full well that the beautifully decorated pots are going permanently into this man's personal collection. "They don't care about dead and gone Indians," a friendly stenographer confesses to him.

Outland's return to the Blue Mesa brings even greater disillusionment when he discovers that his obtuse partner has sold the cliff-dweller relics, not omitting the mummies, to a foreign curio dealer. The site is stripped bare. "There never was any question of money with me, where the mesa and its people were concerned," protests Tom; "I thought we were men enough to keep a trust."[15] His partner is nonplussed, has no comprehension of what has been lost to posterity, had thought of the relics as commodities worthy of being turned into cash, something like a gold mine or a pocketful of turquoise.

The Professor's House may well be Cather's premier expression of pessimism concerning contemporary trends. It suggests no satisfactory explanation for the materialistic fever racing, seemingly unabated, through American society, and it proposes no cure. For Godfrey St. Peter personally, the answer is despair and an impulse toward suicide. But his attempt (perhaps only half conscious) to allow a defective stove to asphyxiate him is thwarted by his well-meaning cleaning woman. No such easy escape is possible. He decides to live, though life has lost its savor. "He had never learned to live without delight," writes Cather; "And he would have to learn to."[16]

My Mortal Enemy

Cather had always responded to the urge to offer stories that were somewhat offbeat, different from the expected and the usual, and so she seldom repeated herself. This urge to test the untrodden path is well demonstrated in Cather's offering for 1926, *My Mortal Enemy*. A slight volume, little more than a novelette in length, and by far the briefest of all of Cather's book-length fiction, *My Mortal Enemy* today is regularly thought of and referred to as the quintessential practical example of the theories given general circulation later (1936, in *Not Under Forty*) in her brief essay "The Novel Démeublé." Here Cather speaks of the distinction between the novel written as amusement and the novel offered as art. Centered upon the principle of selection, a characteristic of art, not of nature, the essay dismisses the overfurnished novel made popular by Honoré de Balzac and during Cather's time a favorite form practiced by

many of her realist contemporaries, such as Theodore Dreiser and
Sinclair Lewis. She favors instead the more stripped-down models to be
found in the works of Stephen Crane and, earlier, in the novels of
Nathaniel Hawthorne.

A novel crowded with the details of everyday existence, no matter
how brilliant, could scarcely be more than a form of journalism, Cather
insisted, and would never be much more than a catalog stuffed full of
ready-made furniture. Cather expressed her preference for writing that
suggests rather than lists, that implies much more than it ever states, for
pages on which things can be felt distinctly even though they are never
specifically named. To employ a term made popular much later, her theory described a form of literary minimalism, which might be summed up
in a reference she had used many times before, going back even to her
college days when she worked as a newspaper drama critic: a reminder
from the elder Alexandre Dumas that to make a drama, one needs little
more than a single passion and four walls.

My Mortal Enemy presents a "heroine" who is the diametric opposite of
those Valkyrie-like women who dominate the novels of 1913–18. Rather
than deifying a woman who places work or art or generous living above
money, Cather undertakes the portrait of one who, trying desperately to
convince herself that her primary concern is love, is forced to realize that
her essential passion has always concerned money. Myra Driscoll has
been warned by her wealthy great-uncle and guardian against marrying
the handsome and well-mannered Oswald Henshawe, who, despite his
fine personal attributes, possesses neither brilliance nor wealth. John
Driscoll speaks plainly, well aware of his niece's weakness for luxuries.
"It's better to be a stray dog in this world than a man without money,"
he warns Myra; "I've tried both ways, and I know. A poor man stinks,
and God hates him."[17] It's hard to speak plainer than that. But the
rebellious young Myra, knowing that she may well be disinherited,
elopes with Oswald nonetheless.

The long aftermath to their wedding—marry in haste, repent at
leisure—forms a chronicle of mounting regret. But the reader is dis-
tanced from the unsavory details—which might have been massive—
through Cather's use of a first-person narrator who sees Myra and
Oswald only at scattered moments in their long history together. Nellie
Birdseye is 15 and finishing high school in Parthia, Illinois, when Myra
comes back to her hometown for the first and only time, more than two
decades after her (financially) disastrous marriage. Later, on a trip to
New York with her Aunt Lydia, a girlhood friend of Myra's, Nellie is

introduced to the Sheridan Square region of Manhattan, an area "then at the parting of the ways" in the city's relentless march northward, a district that is half commercial and half social. Here Myra and Oswald Henshawe live in a "little apartment," a second-floor walk-up in an old brownstone. The genteel poverty of the place is lost completely on the inexperienced Nellie, to whom every detail of that apartment seems "absolutely individual and unique, even the dinner service; the thick grey plates and the soup tureen painted with birds and big, bright flowers—[she] was sure there were no others like them in the world."[18]

Proud in her poverty, Myra overcompensates by means of a reckless squandering of what little cash she has at hand, buying expensive trinkets or hothouse flowers and handing out egregiously generous tips. On one occasion, after Myra has surprised their hansom-cab driver with a tip that is obviously far too large, she confides to Nellie in a rare moment of insight, "It's very nasty, being poor!"[19] Myra is 45 at the time of this encounter, and 10 years elapse before Nellie encounters the Henshawes again, this time in San Francisco. Their finances are shakier than ever. In New York, Oswald had served as private secretary to the president of a railroad. But the line has failed, and Oswald now works six days a week at a nine-to-five job, a lowly position, ill-paid, with the company that runs the local streetcars.

The Henshawes now live in a seedy apartment hotel "wretchedly built and already falling to pieces, although it was new."[20] Here they are surrounded by the worn and tattered remains of their New York furnishings. Myra is already ill with the cancer that will kill her, and she has been twisted by the revenge life has worked on her for impetuous decisions made in youth. A grotesque now, confined to a wheelchair, Myra has become "a witty and rather wicked old woman, who hated life for its defeats [and whose] dry, exultant chuckle . . . seemed to say, 'Ah-ha, I have one more piece of evidence, one more, against the hideous injustice God permits in this world.'"[21]

Of her tarnished romance with Oswald and the marriage she has come to regret so bitterly, Myra says to Nellie, "Oh, if youth but knew!" Their impetuosity has been the ruin of them both. "We've destroyed each other, I should have stayed with my uncle. It was money I needed. We've thrown our lives away."[22] Tamed by life, Myra has come to admitting the truth of her uncle's saying that God hates a poor man. If nothing else, money could be "a protection, a cloak [that could] buy one quiet and some sort of dignity."[23] Most regrettable of all, Myra has now turned on her one-time lover, Oswald, he of the undying devotion and impeccable manners. Oswald is still devoted, entirely so, to his wife's comfort. But in Myra's jaundiced eyes, he has become the author of all her misery, and her dying rebuke to fate is the story's famous and, to many readers, highly ambiguous final line: "Why must I die like this, alone with my mortal enemy!"[24]

With *My Mortal Enemy* Willa Cather had come 180 degrees from her first novels, with their irrepressible and life-loving heroines. The modern woman, like the modern age, inevitably suffered by comparison with those earlier and so much happier models. It was painful for Cather to contemplate the sad diminution of life that the years had brought—so painful that the present era, along with its Myra Driscoll Henshawes, would from now on be viewed by her obliquely, if at all, would be seen only from vantage points placed strategically—and safely—in the past.

Death Comes for the Archbishop

In most Cather novels of the 1920s, the central actors are victimized: Claude Wheeler by the Great War of 1914–18; Marian Forrester by the loss of her great protector-husband; Godfrey St. Peter by a depressive crisis of midlife; Myra Driscoll Henshawe by a youthful error and the vengeful power move of her intransigent old uncle. But in mid-decade Cather turned back to the indomitable hero, and in order to make this work for her, it was essential to forswear the wasteland of postwar American society entirely and turn instead to the far historical past.

The long history of the Roman Catholic church in the American Southwest had been a mixture of successes and failures, but Father Jean Marie Latour, the hero of *Death Comes for the Archbishop*, manages to avoid the grievous errors of certain of his predecessors without compromising his own lofty aims. He manages to create his "great diocese" from the destruction wrought by centuries of neglect. "The old mission churches are in ruins,"[25] says a cardinal, quite frankly—and accurately. The problem never seemed more difficult. Priests are few, those possessed of the proper discipline even fewer. Religious observances have been all but suspended. Offenses against Holy Orders, such as concubinage, are open and notorious. The new vicar to be appointed must possess formidable qualifications—youth, health, zeal, intelligence, even wisdom—for he will be contending against savagery, ignorance, hypocrisy, and religio-political intrigue.

The French Jesuit who is selected—Father Latour—is equal to the challenge. The authorities who send him to America understand full well that his will be no easy life; they know that the Southwest will do what it can to "drink up his youth and strength" even as the desert soil soaks up the rain. Wisely, Latour begins by observing and analyzing. From this acquired knowledge, he is able to array the priests of his diocese into two opposing ranks, their places determined by whether the men have proven to be trusty captains or despicable traitors to their vows; whether, essentially, they have lived *for* the people or *upon* them. Latour's diagnosis of his diocese as a blighted tree is apt. A good arborist, he understands that its only cure may be the timely amputation of its rotten limbs. This cure he attempts to apply, aided by the fortuitous arrival of a vicar so much like himself as to be a moral twin: Father Joseph Vaillant. Vaillant is not much less than a saint, and the fortitude of a saint is what is called for. As Latour's agent, Vaillant assumes the lifetime task of combating those pernicious elements that brutalize life in the southwestern territory and replacing them with humanizing forces.

The struggle of Latour and Vaillant also describes the plot line of the novel. Vaillant's integrity can be measured by the account of his funeral, held outdoors under a great canvas tent because no building in the Denver of his day could accommodate the unprecedented crowds of mourners. Some years afterward, the funeral of Latour—by now the archbishop of Santa Fe—establishes the same point, as his body lies in state before the high altar of the cathedral that he built and that will serve as his tomb. But that plot proceeds in anything but a straight line, for *Death Comes for the Archbishop* is perhaps Cather's most discursive novel, swinging abruptly to left and to right as it describes a zigzag path, including any number of significant time lapses in its progress from start to finish. Along the way it hesitates in order to embrace stories that in themselves amount to discrete tales. Three of these concern contemporary rogue priests, Padres Gallego of Albuquerque, Martinez of Taos, and Lucero of Arroyo Hondo. A fourth concerns the legend of another rogue, Friar Balthazar of Acoma, and of the Indian revolt that had nearly ended forever the history of the Church on that high mesa. And there is the discrete tale of the proud beauty Dona Isabella Olivares, from whom Latour must somehow coax the reluctant truth concerning her age or else lose the generous bequest directed to the Church by her deceased husband.

The novel depicts also the history of the native Indian tribes, their intuitive understanding of the land, and their gentle stewardship of it. The Indians are free of the European need to master nature, to rearrange and re-create it. They hunt but do not slaughter; they use the rivers and forests but do not ravage them; they know the sacred value of water and diligently conserve it. Artistic and peace loving, as seen by Cather, the Indians have no wish to plunder, no ambition even to leave their "Kilroy" on the land. They value instead the ability to pass through water like fish or through air like birds, leaving behind them an undisturbed universe. This view of the past allows Cather to emphasize once more her theme of the increasing and malignant materialism of white commercial/industrial civilization as it encroaches upon and then openly conflicts with the traditional ways of the Indian past.

Death Comes for the Archbishop springs less from personal memories than many other Cather novels do, but in the large sense she was inspired by her many sojourns in the Southwest. The novel is permeated with her love for the countryside and her admiration for its native peoples. For details, she was able to reach back into her considerable bag of memories from her visits of 1912 and 1915. Cather's sense of wonder at the civilizations created by the cliff dwellers once again furnishes food for fiction, especially in her account of the Indian ruins in Canyon de Chelly, similar to those that had so thrilled her at Mesa Verde. And Cather's account of Father Latour's night spent at the pueblo of Isleta in "The Mass at Acoma" is nearly identical in its details to descriptions mailed to her friends on her own visit there in 1912, even to the parrot-filled garden tended by the aged missionary priest.

Memories aside, the novel is based primarily on the life story of Father Jean Baptiste Lamy, first archbishop of Santa Fe. Here Cather relied greatly upon a small volume of history and biography entitled *Life of the Right Reverend Joseph Priest Machebeuf, D.D., Pioneer Priest of Ohio, of Colorado, and Utah, and First Bishop of Denver.* The book, written by the Reverend W. J. Howlett, had been privately published in Pueblo, Colorado, in 1908. Father Joseph Machebeuf is recognized as being the model for Father Joseph Vaillant, Latour's faithful right arm, and Howlett's account included translations from the French of a number of letters written by Machebeuf to his nun sister, Soeur Philomene, in Riom, France, between 1839 and 1886, letters that provided a good many of the historical and biographical details used by Cather in re-creating fictionally the closely interwoven clerical and personal lives of Machebeuf (Vaillant) and Lamy (Latour).

Death Comes for the Archbishop was published to a chorus of praise, even from critics who questioned whether the book was a novel at all or was instead some new form of historical chronicle. Critic Burton Rascoe's declaration that the book was worth reading for the constant enjoyment of its prose alone may have overstated the case, but it recognized the general opinion that Cather had refined her linguistic instrument into a style that was at once simple and subtle, evocative and flexible, and above all, lucid. Looking back, it is clear that Willa Cather in 1927 had reached the apogee of her accomplishment as a writer. That fact inheres also in the contemporary assessment of her career, which had been striding forward ever since 1913 and *O Pioneers!* In 1922 the British writer Hugh Walpole had conducted a poll that placed Cather among the six most important living American writers.[26] By 1929 the poll of critics reported on in the *English Journal* rated Cather the top novelist in the nation.[27] A good deal of credit for this spurt to the front must be given to the overwhelming success of *Death Comes for the Archbishop*. Rebecca West honored Cather in a major essay entitled, appropriately, "The Classic Artist," and the American critic T. K. Whipple, in answer to the question whether or not an artist could exist in the United States, replied simply, "Go read Miss Cather."[28]

Chapter Five
The Final Novels, 1930–1940

Miss Cather has never once tried to see contemporary life as it is; she sees only that it lacks what the past, at least in her idealization of it, had. Thus she has been barred from the task that has occupied most of the world's great artists, the expression of what is central and fundamental in her own age.

Granville Hicks, 1933

During the 1930s, Cather produced only three novels, and although all of them were enthusiastically purchased and widely read by the considerable audience she had attracted, none of the three served significantly to advance her career and, in fact, all three were—and are now—regarded as representing something of a decline in her powers. This may not be surprising when one considers that Cather was nearly 60 as the decade opened, not in the best of health, either physically or psychologically, and that, even more important possibly, the Great Depression had caused societal disruptions that radically affected the way influential critics judged her work.

Shadows on the Rock

The novel with which Cather opened the depression decade, *Shadows on the Rock*, is built in much the same manner as, and from materials similar to, those used in *Death Comes for the Archbishop*. As she gradually retreated from what she saw as the unpleasantries of industrial society, Cather had compensated by forming an admiring attachment to French-Canadian Quebec, much the same as she had formed in 1912–15 to the American Southwest. Again it was the past, rather than the present, that she considered to have been glorious, and for her new story she traveled back in time a good deal further than she had for her story of Archbishop Latour and Father Vaillant, to the turn of the eighteenth century, the days of the original governor of Quebec, Count de Frontenac.

The great Frontenac is the patron of the considerably more lowly central figure, apothecary Euclide Auclair, come to the American continent in order to initiate a new life, one that will not be a mere replica of life in France but an idealized version of it, as free as possible from the materialistic trends that have prevailed at home and that will eventuate in bloody revolution and the execution of Louis XVI. The religious strands in the novel are strong. Cather's life was becoming more and more steadily oriented toward conventional religion—in 1922 she formally, with her parents, joined the Episcopal church in Nebraska—and she saw historic Quebec with much the same eyes as she had seen the American Southwest in the time of the Spanish missions. Cather had described the New Mexican mesas as resembling cathedrals, and in Quebec she found another tall rock, this one situated beside running water, a rock that with its clustered buildings could be imagined as taking on the outlines of an immense chapel.

Members of religious orders play significant roles in *Shadows on the Rock*, and all serve as role models in this revivified and improved version of French life. Bishop Laval, for one, gives away his possessions, his revenues, and his lands in order to live in "naked poverty." The martyr Noël Chabanel chooses to live among the savage Hurons and devote himself to their salvation. Jeanne Le Ber, daughter of Montreal's richest merchant, withdraws from material comfort to cloistered austerity; she elects to live in a barren cell whose four walls enclose the reclusive world wherein she prays and knits for the poor. These people, all of them, are engaged in atoning for the sins of the human race. They live not in the contemporary universe but in a rarefied spiritual universe far removed from the mundane ebb and flow of daily existence.

But layman Euclide Auclair does exist within the society of his time. Widowed and with a daughter, Cécile, to raise, he does his best to create for the two of them an ideal French family life, one of rigorous order and care, as opposed to the carelessness and loss of tradition that characterize so many of the lives surrounding theirs. Much of the story is concerned with the extremely wide contrasts that dramatize the gulf between Auclair's household and the households of others. When young Cécile, for instance, visits the Harnois family on the Ile d'Orleans, she notes at once the coarseness of their cuisine, food prepared without thought and served without pleasantries. The failure of management seen at the Harnoises's comes as a shocking contrast to daily life as Cécile has experienced it in her own home. Their bread is spoiled with too much lard, but no one seems to mind, indeed to notice. Mme Harnois prepares breakfast in her nightcap because she has not troubled to arrange her hair—a trifle, but a significant one to the fastidious Cécile.

In such trifles are found the seeds of barbarism. The Harnois girls sleep in the clothes they have worn all day at play, and they do not bother to wash from their legs the mud splashes or bloody mosquito bites accumulated during daylight hours. Soiled sheets go unchanged for weeks and cause Cécile to reflect on the careful way "her mother had always made everything at home beautiful, just as here everything about cooking, eating, sleeping, living seemed repulsive."[1] Cécile, striving to carry on the practices and traditions so precious to her parents, notes that the utensils of everyday existence—pots and pans, brooms and clouts and brushes—were tools with which people shaped their existence: "One made a climate within a climate; one made days,—the complexion, the special flavour, the special happiness of each day as it passed; one made life."[2]

In 1931 it may well have been that far too many people in the disastrously broken American economy were having an impossibly rough time making any kind of life at all for themselves and their families to be overly concerned about demanding that life be lived on their own terms. In any case, concern over changing bedsheets every two weeks (which had been Mme Auclair's deathbed instruction to her daughter) had in all too many instances yielded precedence to finding a job to work, a house to afford, food to set on the table. Friendly reviewers (and most were yet that in Cather's case) found themselves rather uneasily admiring *Shadows on the Rock* more for its art than for its substance. The writing itself—the classic prose—was as superb as always, but to many the book seemed thin in story, undramatic, and, at its worst, dull.

Hostile critics, especially those now espousing the Marxist principle of class struggle, were busily promoting fiction as a tool of social reform. This faction made Cather a specific target of attack. Cather's opposition was led by Granville Hicks, who used his review of *Shadows on the Rock* to propose that Cather, despite exaggerated claims made in the past, was not and never had been anything more than "a minor artist." It took stern stuff to be a novelist, said Hicks, and Cather's work had always been flawed by an unserviceable softness. By devoting herself now to a re-creation of the distant past while ignoring the social exigencies of the present, he argued, Cather had betrayed her talent. Her new novel was merely a symptom of her flight from the present, and that kind of flight, said Hicks, "is and always has been destructive of the artistic virtues."[3] She had made herself irrelevant.

Despite the onslaught, older viewpoints on Cather prevailed for the time being. *Shadows on the Rock* became a runaway best-seller, and *Time* magazine expressed the predominating opinion that Willa Cather could not possibly write a bad novel by placing her photograph on its cover and praising her work in a long congratulatory story, with a low bow to publisher Alfred A. Knopf, who, said the magazine, had every reason in the world to be "pleased and proud to be purveyor of what is sure to be acclaimed as a Good Book written by an obviously home-grown author."[4]

Lucy Gayheart

Alfred A. Knopf issued Willa Cather's eleventh novel in August 1935. Previous to this, the story had been serialized in the *Woman's Home Companion*, one of the most popular of the mass-circulation magazines that then dominated the American print media, and many later critics have been content to let the novel remain in the popular domain where it first met the public's eye, dismissing it, usually, with a few kind but perfunctory comments as if somehow it had managed to creep into the Cather canon by error.

For *Lucy Gayheart* Cather returned to her Nebraska materials and her memories of Red Cloud and its people. The title character was based, Cather admitted, on a local girl and the name Gayheart came from her memory of a young woman whom Cather had known only briefly in Blue Hill, Nebraska, but whose personality had impressed her mightily, and whose name she recalled as Miss Gayhardt. For the first time, Cather structured a novel according to a variation of the triangle plot. Lucy, going to Chicago in about 1898 to study music, is loved by the hometown banker's son, Harry Gordon, tall, handsome, eight years older than she, and just a bit obtuse. Lucy reciprocates some of Harry's feelings, even though she seems to intuit that his attraction is motivated by a deep desire "to have a wife other men would envy him."[5] In Chicago, Lucy becomes deeply infatuated with Clement Sebastian, the singer for whom she plays piano accompaniment. Sebastian is 50 and unhappily married. He has lived apart from his wife for many years.

During a visit to Chicago in the early spring of 1902, Harry Gordon proposes to Lucy. "We know each other pretty well," is the matter-of-fact manner in which he begins: "You've had your little fling. . . . Why waste any more time? This is April; I should think we might be married in May. Oh, June, if you like!"[6] This sounds a good deal more like a business proposition than a marriage proposal, and Lucy is justifiably infuriated, so much so that she reveals that she is in love with Sebastian, and further (a lie), that she has been sexually intimate with him. This settles the matter. His male pride hurt, Harry Gordon washes his hands of Lucy, then marries on the rebound, his moneyed wife a good business deal but not a woman he can ever love deeply. Then Sebastian is drowned in a boating accident on Lake Como in Italy, and the heartbroken Lucy retreats to Nebraska, where she attempts unsuccessfully to mend her fences with Harry Gorden before she herself drowns while skating on the thin ice of the Platte River.

Lucy Gayheart is easy reading, a well-written piece of fiction dominated by a deep, sad sense of nostalgia for a past that is gone and cannot be recovered. The years covering the central action, 1901 and 1902, are framed by a treatment of Lucy's hometown some 25 or 30 years following her death—what at the moment of Cather's writing would have been "the present" of the novel, the early 1930s. The note of wistful remembrance is introduced in the very opening lines of the story: "In Haverford on the Platte the townspeople still talk of Lucy Gayheart. They do not talk of her a great deal, to be sure; life goes on and we live in the present. But when they do mention her name it is with a gentle glow in the face or the voice, a confidential glance which says: 'Yes, you, too, remember?' They still see her as a slight figure always in motion; dancing or skating, or walking swiftly with intense direction, like a bird flying home."[7] The coda to the novel (book 3) dwells primarily upon the death and funeral of Lucy's father, and the sense of infinite regret of soul with which Harry Gordon faces the remainder of his life, seeing himself, in a sense, as the sole survivor of the Gayheart family, all dead and gone: "now the story was finished: no grandchildren, complete oblivion."[8] Except for memory, of course, where the legend of Lucy Gayheart lodges, calling to mind a girl "so young, so lovely, and, everybody knew, so unhappy [that she seemed like] a bird being shot down when it rises in its morning flight toward the sun."[9]

In the end of the Gayheart family line, Harry Gordon, himself involved in a barren marriage, foresees the end of his own line of descent. Sentimentally, he takes regular Sunday-afternoon walks out to the old Gayheart place on the edge of town; and sentimentally, he takes measures to ensure the preservation of the cement sidewalk containing the imprints of Lucy's feet left there as a child, long ago when the walk was laid. The sentimentality of this extended coda is matched again and again during the story proper, whose pages are replete with experiences of loss and vain regret. There is Sebastian's midlife mourning for a youth "forever and irrevocably gone," and his remark to Lucy upon observing her joy over a vase of mimosa: "Yes, they're nice, aren't they? Very suggestive: youth, love, hope—all the things that pass." There is Lucy's own reaction to the death of Sebastian, a man she cannot hope ever to marry and who seems much too bound up in his own dark weltschmerz to reciprocate even a fraction of her feelings; she is said to have had her "heart frozen and [her] world destroyed in a moment."[10] In a sense, Lucy dedicates the remainder of her brief life to her sorrow.

And above all of this sadness hovers the aging author, nostalgically evoking details of small-town experience, "the way it was" in Red Cloud, Nebraska, when the century turned. Many of these details ring true, as they so often do in Cather's work, for she was an authority on the topic. But most of this local color had already been utilized, and to better purpose, during the earlier appearances in her fiction of Red Cloud, the generic small town, appearing under names such as Black Hawk, Sweet Water, Hanover, Moonstone, and Frankfort. Lucy's pursuit of music studies in Chicago is a reprise of *The Song of the Lark* written small, and Lucy is not represented as possessed of anything even remotely resembling the intense desire, determination, talent, and sheer grit that make Thea Kronborg's story so compelling. Indeed, Cather says of Lucy that she "never dreamed of a 'career.'" Being dominated by a devotion to her feelings rather than her ambition, she is "too careless and light-hearted to take herself very seriously."[11] And that has been the way scholars, with good reason, have treated Lucy's story, as a novel of pleasant diversion but not to be taken very seriously.

Sapphira and the Slave Girl

At the end of the 1930s, perhaps the last period of time in which she remained capable of completing a sustained work of fiction, Cather produced her final novel. Her work had often relied upon memories from the past, but for *Sapphira and the Slave Girl* she reached back considerably beyond her own Red Cloud girlhood, to the very earliest pictures imprinted on her mind, coming from her childhood days in the Virginia she had left when she was 10 years old.

Hidden in Cather's distant southern past was a subject well worth treating, the dark secret of slavery that, to Cather, represented the ultimate crime of private ownership. The Cathers of Winchester had broken apart over this issue, like many another border-state family in the 1860s, and in time the quarrel had eventuated in the removal of certain Cathers to Nebraska. But by the 1930s, the intrafamily quarrel was long over, buried—if not forgotten—and Cather was impelled to write her story of a family broken on the wheel of human bondage.

This family, the Colberts, includes principally Henry, the miller; his wife, Sapphira; and their daughter, Rachel Blake. Sapphira, the slave owner, is born into a society erected upon the fact of ownership and dedicated to its preservation. She is a woman of iron determination, and her right to do with her slaves whatever she chooses is to her a privilege ordained by heaven. But her husband's mind is troubled and has been troubled ever since the day of his marriage into a slave-owning family. That his Bible appears to yield him no unequivocal condemnation of slavery causes him much mental distress. Slavery is a barrier between Sapphira and her daughter Rachel also; but Rachel finds herself equally disturbed and confused by the readiness with which the blacks appear to accept their bondage. She observes her mother believing wholeheartedly in slavery; the slaves themselves seeming to believe in it. Still, for Rachel, "it ain't right." In the background are heard other voices, pro and con. Sapphira's relatives form a solid front to guard their property rights. Pitted against them in that Virginia neighborhood are the Bywater family and various Quakers. In this uneasy context one senses the earth begin to rumble as the abolitionist crusade of the 1850s gets under way.

Sapphira is no polemic, but the dismal effects of bondage on the human spirit are graphically presented. There are many examples. One meets Jezebel, betrayed by slave-hunting members of her own African tribe. The brutal ocean passage of the crowded slave ship is sketched. One meets Till, Sapphira's house servant, arbitrarily wed to a "capon man" as an imposed birth control measure. One meets especially the Colberts themselves, a family crippled by dissension.

The opening scene of the novel involves a quarrel. Sapphira is determined to barter her slave girl Nancy to a neighbor; her husband curtly declares, "We don't sell our people," and he will not place his required signature on the deed of sale, thus tying Sapphira's hands. Rachel also resists the transaction: "A feeling long smothered had blazed up in her— had become a conviction. She had never heard the thing said before, never put into words. It was the *owning* that was wrong, the relation itself, no matter how convenient or agreeable it might be for master or servant."[12]

In her anger at being thwarted, Sapphira is susceptible to malicious gossip that would link her husband's opposition with the possibility that his interest in Nancy is sexual. To circumvent Henry's steadfast opposition, Sapphira devises her own roundabout means of ridding herself of the slave girl, now regarded as a threat to her marriage. She will expose Nancy to her houseguest, a dissolute young cousin, knowing full well that rape will be the probable outcome. The act of miscegenation accomplished, the mores of the time and place will then demand Nancy's expulsion from the premises. But knowledge of this cynical plot prompts Rachel to connive with her father to see that Nancy is smuggled north through the Underground Railroad to Canada and freedom. This act of filial defiance severs the mother-daughter bond and prefigures the divisions that loom ahead in the approaching outbreak of hostilities between North and South.

In *Sapphira* Cather dispenses with protagonists eager for personal success (Thea, Alexandra) or preoccupied with their emotions (Lucy) and instead concentrates her attention on people who, like the heroes of her religious novels (Latour, Auclair), place principle above self or society above family. She returns not only to her very earliest childhood memory—the return, years afterward, of the former slave Nancy to the Cather home in Virginia—but also to one of her earliest and most pervasive themes: the conflict between the spirit and the material. That struggle is signified by Henry Colbert's thumbing through his copy of John Bunyan's *Holy War* for the tale of Mansoul, Diabolus smashing through her gates, and the final reestablishment of Mansoul by Prince Emmanuel. The thought that evil would not triumph finally is pleasantly reassuring to Colbert, and it is this same thought that ultimately is the message of the last book Cather published in her lifetime.

That *Shadows on the Rock*, *Lucy Gayheart*, and *Sapphira and the Slave Girl* are good novels goes almost without saying, and they possess many of the expected merits of Cather's masterworks. But what they lack is crucial: the vibrant, life-giving presence of exciting, fully realized central figures who rivet the attention and cling to the reader's mind long after the book itself has been laid back on the shelf. And if the story is ever to be taken off that shelf again, for rereading, it is most likely to be the enduring appeal of the characters that will prompt the desire to take a second taste.

The enthusiastic reviewers who exclaimed over Cather's creation of Alexandra Bergson and Thea Kronborg, who shouted hosannas when Cather offered them stories dominated by the likes of Marian Forrester and Father Latour, could find no equivalents in Cather's final novels. In 1918 the titanic figure of Ántonia Shimerda so captivated the often-bilious H. L. Mencken that he admonished all the fortunate possessors of her story with a simple imperative: "Don't give this away!"[13] Memorable characters have always stood at the center of great fiction—have been what makes a story great, of course, created people who live and breathe, suffer and struggle, triumph or fail in manners so near to actuality that a reader conceives of them as being actual flesh and blood, empathizing and identifying with them. Cather in *The Song of the Lark* had created just such a group of persons, wrote Frederick Tabor Cooper in his *Bookman* review of that novel, "persons of such strong actuality that we wish to adopt them, as it were, into our own families, take them into our own homes to live with us, as we sometimes do with friends in the real world, because we identify so closely with their hopes and fears.[14]

It was precisely this uncanny, somewhat magical ability to shape passionate, breathing people on the pages of a book that after about 1930 failed Willa Cather, leaving most of her other literary powers intact but stranded without human figures that we identify with and care deeply about. In a sad way, then, these novels of her later years come to resemble elaborate stages set for human actions that never occur.

Chapter Six

Willa Cather's Shorter Fiction: 1892–1948

[Willa Cather's short stories] are stories that lift themselves completely above the level of current American fiction, even of good fiction.

H. L. Mencken, 1920

Although Willa Cather is best known as a novelist, she began—and ended—her career in fiction as an author of short stories. Between 1912 and 1940 she published 12 novels, but for better than 50 years she was a contributor to American magazines, beginning in 1892 when her brief story "Peter" (later called "Peter Sedelack, Father of Anton") appeared in the *Mahogany Tree* in Boston. Cather's last completed work, "The Best Years," was a short story; it appeared posthumously in 1948 in her final collection, *The Old Beauty and Others*.

Apprenticeship: The Bitter Life on the Divide

Cather's first stories clearly were apprentice work at which she learned her trade, and they tended toward being character sketches or local-color attempts, upon which a semblance of plot had been imposed, sometimes rather arbitrarily. "Peter," "Lou, the Prophet" (1892), and "Nanette: An Aside" (1897) are representative. Others were experiments in a variety of genres then experiencing a rush of popularity. "A Tale of the White Pyramid" (1892), for instance, is an attempt at the historical fantasy, just as "A Night at Greenway Court" (1896) apes the historical romance. Following the success of Bret Harte and Rudyard Kipling, stories of the "heathen Chinee" were in vogue, written and published in droves; and Cather, undeterred by the fact that she knew precious little about either Asian ethnics or the city of San Francisco, tried her hand at least twice on stories of immigrant Chinese. While she was still in college, Cather's "A Son of the Celestial" (1893) appeared in the campus magazine the *Hesperian*, and seven years later "The Conversion of Sun Loo" was published in the *Library* in Pittsburgh. "The Fear That Walks by Noonday"

(1894)—idea by Cather's campus friend Dorothy Canfield, writing by Cather herself—is an uneasy blend of the ghost story and the campus football story.

Because Cather, while working for small Pittsburgh magazines such as the *Library* and the *Home Monthly*, was more often than not left to fend for herself in securing material to fill their pages, she ended up by writing most of some of the issues practically by herself, using a half-dozen or more aliases to disguise the fact. It was to be expected that a good deal of potboiling fiction might be the result, and that is precisely what did occur. The decade between 1892 and 1902 is littered with failed experiments that the mature Cather later regretted, rightly, and that she did her best, again rightly, to abandon, to forget, and then to suppress.

Here and there, however, shining like bright needles in drab haystacks, are pieces of fiction that bear Willa Cather's name and still live. Some of these continue to read amazingly well. Invariably, these are works in which the young author gropes her unsteady way toward her most natural subject matter: Nebraska during the 1880s. "You have your Nebraska materials" is what her mentor Sarah Orne Jewett was telling Cather as late as 1908, chiding her gently but unmistakably for not yet having thoroughly mined that streak of rich literary ore. The young Cather, like many literary aspirants before and after, was wildly excited by the prospect of doing something "different," something "imaginative" or "creative," and so spent a good deal of herself striking out experimentally in various unfruitful directions, sometimes in imitation of writers whose accomplishment she admired but with whom she did not necessarily share much in common.

When Cather did turn for material to her Nebraska girlhood in a really serious manner, the result was almost always fiction that even today is immediate and gripping. Early works may sometimes suffer from lack of form and proper development, but they still retain something of value for the contemporary reader. "Peter," that first published story, is one of these successes, "Lou, the Prophet" another. Both stories concern grotesque strands of life on the Nebraska Divide, and both were published while Cather was a university student. In the year following her graduation, her directly titled story "On the Divide" appeared in the nationally circulated magazine *Overland Monthly*. It was a landmark story, one clearly pointing the way toward the fiction that after 1912 would make its author famous on a global scale.

In "On the Divide" Cather tells the story of a giant Norwegian set-
tler, Canute Canuteson, whose physical and psychological condition is
pointedly summed up as "the wreck of ten winters on the Divide."
Having endured a solitary life in a log-and-sod shanty, Canute attempts
to flout the derangements a prolonged bout of loneliness can induce.
"Insanity and suicide are very common things on the Divide," comments
Cather, for once letting herself go, striking out boldly at targets in her
natural element; "They come on like an epidemic in the hot wind season.
Those scorching dusty winds that blow up over the bluffs from Kansas
seem to dry up the blood in men's veins as they do the sap in the corn
leaves."[1] Such lines, such metaphors, could come only from one who
knew intimately that which she was writing about; and Cather, who had
the experience of 10 years in Red Cloud, just a mere handful of miles
from the Kansas line, surely did. With "On the Divide" Cather might be
said to have come of age as a writer.

East Is East: *The Troll Garden*

During her lifetime, Cather arranged for the publication of three collections of her short fiction. The first of these was *The Troll Garden* (1905),
whose content at once revealed the tug-of-war going on between the
two strands of subject matter that forever would struggle to dominate
Cather's attention as a writer: those early days in Nebraska and the difficult way of the artist. Seven recent stories constitute the collection, all of
them published since 1903, four receiving magazine publication prior to
The Troll Garden and the others receiving their first publication with the
collection.

The contents of the stories do much to reveal the interesting and
somewhat compulsive manner in which Cather's twin themes both dominate her attention and interweave with one another. Some of the stories,
such as "Flavia and Her Artists," "The Garden Lodge," and "The
Marriage of Phaedra," not only concentrate upon the artistic life but are
very much stories of the American urban East; others, such as "`A
Death in the Desert'" and "The Sculptor's Funeral," while given a western setting, concern artists whose productive lives were altogether identified with eastern locales. Conversely, "A Wagner Matinee," while set in
the East, is decidedly a western story. In such tales as these, the West
invariably represents for Cather a society that is philistine to its core,
crass, pragmatic, closed, and both distrustful and unappreciative of art.

The East, on the other hand, is sophisticated, open, welcoming, and considerably more prepared to recognize and reward artistic endeavor.

In a general way, then, the West is "bad," the East "good." Such a generality appears to summarize attitudes Cather had been developing since at least adolescence, attitudes that had both sustained and troubled her in Pittsburgh as she considered her own loyalties, split as they were between her love and hate for Nebraska (where she feared her fate might be to die in a cornfield) and her attraction to the East, which she needed for her artistic development but where the competition for real critical acclaim was fearsome.

"Paul's Case" is set in the East and is allied most closely with the stories of art, except that its protagonist is only a pretend artist, a poor, talentless, deluded adolescent who is captivated by the make-believe he encounters as an usher at Pittsburgh's Carnegie Hall. Under that influence he embezzles money for a wild, brief indulgence in New York City. In the immediate aftermath of his crazy fling, touched at last by the horrifying reality of what he has done, he throws himself under the wheels of a locomotive. The story is the work of an expert, and its theme of the difficult passage from youth to maturity is universal. "Paul's Case," for many years the favorite selection representing Cather in anthologies, still makes regular appearances in collections of "great" American stories.

"'A Death in the Desert'" exemplifies the curious ways in which Cather's two themes sometimes blend. Set within a western locale, it concerns an opera singer, Katherine Gaylord, native of Bird City, Iowa, who lies on her deathbed in Cheyenne, Wyoming, apparently a victim of tuberculosis. Certain of Cather's remarks, offered through Katherine's westerner brother, highlight the tension between the East-West thematic dichotomy: "She had to fight her own way from the first. She got [away from the West] to Chicago, and then to New York, and then to Europe, where she went up like lightning, and got a taste for it all; and now she's dying here like a rat in a hole, out of her own world, and she can't fall back into ours."[2] Its western setting notwithstanding, the bulk of the story concerns eastern artistic careers and world concert tours. Probably not by accident, it joins "Flavia and Her Artists," "The Garden Lodge," and "The Marriage of Phaedra"—the other stories of artistic life—as having demonstrated only the most minimal ability to attract or hold readers over time.

On the other hand, the three western stories appearing in *The Troll Garden* have enjoyed continuous critical respect and are considered today to hold their own with no difficulty among Cather's masterworks. "The Sculptor's Funeral" takes up more directly the theme implicit in "'A Death in the Desert,'" the impossibility of fulfilling artistic yearnings in a frontier society. Its hero is a young sculptor, Harvey Merrick, who has died, like Katherine Gaylord, of tuberculosis. In order to establish a promising career in the East, Merrick had to—and had managed to— escape from the depressing environment of his antiartistic Kansas village. But now he is dead and his coffin has been shipped by freight to the town he loathed—and where he was loathed in turn by a group of hometown citizens, philistines every one, who had never understood him and who, if they had, would have done everything possible to dissuade him from his chosen life's work.

One of these locals, speaking of the dead sculptor as a failure, with no sense of irony suggests that he could possibly have been saved by being sent as a youth to a first-rate business school in Kansas City. It is only the lawyer, Jim Laird (Cather's persona in the story), who deflates this criticism with his indignant protest: "Harvey Merrick wouldn't have given one sunset over your marshes for all you've got put together, and you know it."[3] Sarah Orne Jewett told Cather that "The Sculptor's Funeral" marked her finest achievement to that date.

"A Wagner Matinee," like "The Sculptor's Funeral," is a no-holds-barred, even bitter portrayal of the closed-in life on the Divide. Aunt Georgiana (based on Cather's Aunt Franc Cather), has long ago renounced her dreams of a musical future in favor of married life on the Divide. For 30 years she has lived in veritable exile, to the point of forgetting entirely that early dream. But after a visit to Boston, where her nephew treats her to a concert of Wagnerian music, Aunt Georgiana comes to realize the enormity of what she has lost and, worse, the impossibility of ever recouping any of her dreams. Following her afternoon of rapture in the concert hall, the departure of the orchestra comes upon her like a summons of death. "I don't want to go, Clark," she sobs; "I don't want to go."[4] From memories of his own Nebraska boyhood, her nephew knows precisely what she means, knows that "just outside the concert hall, lay the black pond with the cattle-tracked bluffs, the tall, unpainted house, with weather-curled boards; naked as a tower, the crook-backed ash seedlings where the dish-cloths hung to dry; the gaunt, molting turkeys picking up refuse about the kitchen door."[5] The story is one of Cather's most unflinching portrayals of life on the isolated plains, and in its pages she comes as close as she ever did to rejecting the West.

A Life of Art: *Youth and the Bright Medusa*

Between 1905 and 1920, when Cather selected stories for her second collection, she published no less than 17 short stories. For a good portion of this time she was extremely busy, working full-time at *McClure's Magazine* in New York City (where seven of the stories first appeared) and also writing her first four novels. In *Youth and the Bright Medusa* (1920), the first of her books to come from Alfred A. Knopf, Cather reached back 15 years to *The Troll Garden*, intuitively selecting three of its best stories for inclusion in her new collection: "The Sculptor's Funeral," "A Wagner Matinee," and "Paul's Case." The remaining four stories she now considered worth saving were all published in magazines between 1916 and 1920. In shaping *Youth and the Bright Medusa*, Cather chose not to collect most of the short fiction she had published since 1905; many of these stories concerned life in the metropolis, not excluding topics of journalistic life suggested by her work at *McClure's*.

Insofar as Cather was concerned, all of these "rejected" stories were to be consigned to a publishing limbo and forgotten, even though she did at times retain a fondness for some of them and even professed a certain pride of authorship in a few. That handful that Cather did not turn her back upon entirely (and yet chose not to republish) were those that have been most favorably commented upon by Cather scholars in recent times. And all of them are closely allied with Cather's western fiction. The best certainly are these three: "The Joy of Nelly Deane," "The Enchanted Bluff," and "The Bohemian Girl."

"The Joy of Nelly Deane" (1911) represents in some respects the first tentative working out of what eventually (1935) would become the novel *Lucy Gayheart*, and certain of Cather's sentences seem uncannily predictive of the later work: "Every one admitted that Nelly was the prettiest girl in Riverbend [Red Cloud], and the gayest—oh, the gayest!": "Twice she broke through the ice and got soused in the river because she never looked where she skated or cared what happened so long as she went fast enough."[6] Nelly is infatuated with Guy Franklin, tall, carefully groomed, and considerably older than she, a one-sided affair of the heart much like Lucy Gayheart's with Clement Sebastian, one that comes to nothing. And like Lucy, Nelly dies very young, though in different circumstances. But despite such strong similarities, "The Joy of Nelly Deane" has enough going for itself on its own as a story to stand quite independent of the later novel and to exist as a fine reading experience, redolent on every line of Cather's Red Cloud and Webster County, Nebraska.

"The Enchanted Bluff" (1909), even though one of Cather's briefest stories from the period, surely merits the label of "little masterpiece" tied on it by Cather's short-fiction editors, Virginia Faulkner and Mildred R. Bennett.[7] Although Cather in 1909 had not yet visited the Southwest, surely every child of her time, at least those growing up in the neighboring western-midwestern states, had heard tales of the pueblos, the mesa country, and the mysterious cliff dwellers of Arizona and New Mexico. In any event, it was precocious of Cather, even before seeing the southwestern countryside up close for herself, to use the image of the mesa as a sacred and mysterious goal for the first time here in this tale of youthful aspiration combined with adult confinement. On the banks of a sluggish Nebraska river lounge a small group of boyhood friends from Sandtown (yet another nom de plume for Red Cloud). They dream of a legendary mesa beyond the horizon, a "big red rock" emblematic of the youthful desire to seek, to explore, at last to find. Unanimously, the boys resolve individually to make the mesa their common goal. But after a long projection forward in time, the reader learns the sad truth. Of all the resolute young men, not a single one in adulthood has managed to hold to his course. Each has been seduced somehow by the paraphernalia of life, and most have entirely relinquished and even forgotten that old romantic ambition someday to reach the mesa.

The one-time aspirants have been dissuaded from their difficult trek by the pressures of a thing-obsessed, dollar-oriented society that binds their souls to the flat plain. Of one of them Cather (who in 1915 would herself ride on horseback to Mesa Verde) says that he will travel "nowhere that his red touring car cannot go." Her comment speaks for them all. Economical and directly focused, "The Enchanted Bluff" reads like an unpreachy morality tale, and the great wonder is why Willa Cather would think it not worth collecting in more permanent form than the ephemeral pages of the April 1901 issue of *Harper's*, which for half a century was the only place where it might be found.

There is no question that the finest Cather story of the period is "The Bohemian Girl," and the same question applies regarding its not being given assurance of permanence via a collection. When this long story (20,000 words, the length of a good-size novella) was first published in *McClure's Magazine* in 1912, it was enthusiastically received by the magazine's subscribers, and Cather considered combining it in a single vol-

ume with her *O Pioneers!* materials. She decided against this venture, but
she did recognize the close kinship of this story with that of Alexandra
Bergson, both taking place on the Divide during the same time period
covered by the novel. "The Bohemian Girl," aside from being Cather's
first really extended treatment of Norwegian- and Bohemian-immigrant
life, displays the author fully and joyously immersed in her most natural
subject matter. And the story is set not during the frigid and forbidding
wintertime but at the moment of the land's most extreme fruitfulness.
Cather's love for Nebraska is clearly evident: "The moonlight flooded
that great, silent land. The reaped fields lay yellow in it. The straw
stacks and poplar windbreaks threw sharp black shadows. The roads
were white rivers of dust. The sky was a deep, crystalline blue, and the
stars were few and faint. Everything seemed to have succumbed, to have
sunk to sleep, under the great, golden, tender, midsummer moon. The
splendor of it seemed to transcend human life and human fate."[8]

In keeping with such a setting, "The Bohemian Girl" is a love story
concerning the Norwegian Nils Ericson's journey back from Bergen,
where he is an official with a Norwegian shipping line, to the Divide,
where 12 years before he had left his boyhood love, Clara Vavrika,
behind while he sought his fortune. Considerably more mature now and
sobered by life, Nils has come back to claim Clara belatedly. But in the
meantime she has married Nils's brother Olaf, and when Nils broaches
his elopement proposition to Clara, her immediate reply is, "Are you
crazy, Nils? We couldn't go away like that."[9] Not, that is, unless she
were to allow herself to be overcome by the passion she knows she still
experiences in Nils's presence. "The Bohemian Girl" is full of fresh, fully
realized characters and loaded with authentic local color—and it shows
Cather to be a master of both.

All of the four new stories collected in *Youth and the Bright Medusa*
concern the problems of professional musicians—singers—and as a
group they develop the theme of the artist as celebrity, the relationship
to society resulting from the pressure of popular fame, and the personal
cost to the artist exacted by a life devoted to pleasing one's "public." It
was a theme that was gaining currency swiftly in Cather's life, as her
books became ever more widely sold and openly praised, making
demands on her privacy she had not wholly anticipated. It was also a
major strand of the new popular culture that was making headway in
American society generally, where the notion of celebrity was taking
hold with a firm, powerful, and even dictatorial grip.

Two stories best serve to illustrate this strand of Cather's interest as expressed fictionally in *Youth and the Bright Medusa*. "Coming, Aphrodite!" contrasts a pair of artists, first glimpsed during the passionate heat of their youth and then observed during their middle years. Don Hedger is a painter toiling in the avant-garde who insists upon following his own star, declining to produce the same thing over and over, no matter how profitable. Eden Bower is a singer whose ambition for a musical career includes the desire to live well in a big city, to be admired by many men, and to achieve the satisfaction of her every material want. Eden urges Don to paint the types of pictures that conform to popular taste; later, after he has become financially successful, there will be time to paint pictures to please himself. "You know very well there's only one kind of success that's real," Eden says, meaning that measured by dollars.

Following a momentary blaze of romance, doomed by the differences in their characters and sense of values, these two aspirants go their separate ways, to be seen again 18 years later, when both have "succeeded." Don Hedger, the more resolute, has forced the world to recognize his "very modern" canvases; he has not compromised. Eden Bower's name blazes in electric lights above the Lexington Opera House, where she is opening—again—with the Puccini opera she does so well that she rarely dares attempt anything else. She gives the same performance always; her audience can count on its *not* being different. They get what they expect, what they want, what they pay for. While Don Hedger at 40 is "decidedly an influence" in the painting world, his name on the lips of every young person aspiring to excellence, Eden Bower has acquired a huge popular following—and a face that, Cather says, is "hard and settled, like a plaster cast."

"The Diamond Mine" defines another price the artist may be forced to pay if she responds unduly to the claims people make on her personal life. Cressida Garnet has risen to the top ranks of American opera singers after a long struggle, aided by her determination and physical vitality. All thoughts are on perfecting her art. Unlike Eden Bower, Cressida does not feel the need for possessions. But as she matures she finds herself weighted down nevertheless, not by things but by people. One day, at age 42, Cressida wakes up to the realization that her need to have people around her and close to her has victimized her. The emotional freight she carries has been imposed by a series of rapacious husbands and a pack of bilious siblings who regard her somewhat as a natural source, a vein of ore—a "diamond mine"—open for free-wheeling exploitation. It

dawns on Cressida at last: the truth that her personal relationships somehow, despite her hopes, have always involved dollars.

During the 1920s, and later, Cather, fully occupied with her succession of novels, had comparatively little time to spare for short fiction.
From time to time, however, she did try her hand at the short story, and
with varying degrees of success. In 1925 and 1929 Cather published two
longish stories, both inspired by her years in Pittsburgh. The first,
"Uncle Valentine," stems from her feeling for the young composer
Ethelbert Nevin, who died at the age of 37 while she was living there,
and whom she felt to be the outstanding composer of his generation.
The second story, "Double Birthday," evokes memories of Judge Samuel
McClung and Isabelle and the George Seibel home where Cather spent
so many enjoyable Christmas holidays. Both stories are finely crafted and
evocative of Pittsburgh at the turn of the century, but neither furnishes
truly serious competition for Cather's best work.

And West Is West: *Obscure Destinies*

The same complaint cannot be made against Willa Cather's next foray
into the short story, works gathered in the collection entitled *Obscure
Destinies*, which appeared in 1932. The volume contains three stories,
and two of these rank high among Cather's masterworks. Perhaps it is a
matter of coincidence (and perhaps it is not) that both of the stories are
based upon the author's early years in Nebraska. "Old Mrs. Harris" tells
of the relationships between three generations of women of one family
living together in the same small, crowded house:

> The kitchen was hot and empty, full of the untempered afternoon sun. A
> door stood open into the next room; a cluttered, hideous room, yet some-
> how homely. There, beside a goodsbox covered with figured oilcloth,
> stood an old woman in a brown calico dress, washing her hot face and
> neck at a tin basin. She stood with her feet wide apart, in an attitude of
> profound weariness.[10]

This is Old Grandma Harris, a portrait inspired by memories of Cather's
own grandmother, Rachel Boak.

> Victoria might eat all the cookies her neighbor sent in, but she would
> give away anything she had. She was always ready to lend her dresses and
> hats and bits of jewellery for the school theatricals, and she never worked

people for favors. . . . She wasn't in the least willowy or languishing, as
Mrs. Rosen had usually found Southern ladies to be. She was high-spirit-
ed and direct; a trifle imperious, but with a shade of diffidence, too, as if
she were trying to adjust herself to a new group of people and do the
right thing.[11]

This is Victoria Templeton, Old Mrs. Harris's daughter, inspired by
Cather's mother, Virginia Boak Cather.

Vickie went on stumbling through the Latin verses, and Mrs. Rosen sat
watching her. You couldn't tell about Vickie. She wasn't pretty, yet Mrs.
Rosen found her attractive. She liked her sturdy build, and the steady
vitality that glowed in her rosy skin and dark blue eyes,—even gave a
springy quality to her curly reddish-brown hair, which she still wore in a
single braid down her back.[12]

This is Vickie Templeton, Old Mrs. Harris's granddaughter, inspired by
the author's recollections of herself as a girl and the circumstances of that
life. The story concerns Vickie's close friendship with her neighbor Mrs.
Wiener (Mrs. Rosen), who allowed her the run of her library, as well as
her relationships with her mother, her father (Hilary Templeton in the
story), and Mandy, the Harris's bond girl, based upon Margie Anderson,
who had accompanied the George Cather family to Nebraska. The story
is set in Skyline, Colorado, but, again, the initiated reader understands
that the place-name is merely one more pseudonym for Red Cloud,
Nebraska.

Cather wrote few works more grounded in autobiography than "Old
Mrs. Harris," which captures the feel of the time and the place and the
people splendidly. It certified that Cather, at least as the 1930s opened,
when the story was composed, could still write superior works of fiction—provided that they touched the deepest impulses in her writer's
heart.

Equally grounded in Cather's early life and an even better story, perhaps, than "Old Mrs. Harris" is "Neighbour Rosicky," written in 1928.
This extended story exists as a sort of coda to *My Ántonia*, having as its
central figure an immigrant Bohemian farmer, Anton Rosicky, who is
based upon the man whom the real-life Ántonia married, father of her
several children. He makes an appearance in *My Ántonia* in a bit role as
Anton Cuzak, but in the new story he is at center stage, a sturdy, seasoned character who has lived a long and productive life now approaching its end.

Rosicky serves to animate Cather's belief in the individual's power not only to survive but to prevail, to make changes that alter the conditions of life. Rosicky moves twice before settling in Nebraska. He leaves his native Prague for London and then for New York, and he considers both moves to be sorry mistakes. But he is far from feeling—or being—trapped by unfriendly environments. In his case, life offers not only a second chance but a third; and on his third major move, Rosicky discovers, in the Nebraska Divide territory, conditions that he is content to accept as his destiny.

When, at the close of his long life, Rosicky is buried in a private family burial ground close to his cornfields, his physician, Dr. Ed Burleigh, reflects, "Nothing could be more undeathlike than this place; nothing could be more right for a man who had helped to do the work of great cities and had always longed for the open country and had got to it at last. Rosicky's life seemed to him complete and beautiful."[13] "Neighbour Rosicky" is one of the most consistently cheering stories Cather ever published, escaping almost entirely the mournful and bitter note that had characterized her earliest efforts at writing of the difficult life on the Divide. At the present time, it is the most popular choice of anthologists. Cather could do much worse than to be introduced to new readers by way of "Neighbour Rosicky."

The Sad Decline: *The Old Beauty and Others*

When Willa Cather died in 1947 she had on hand a trio of completed short fictional works. "Before Breakfast" is a triviality, and "The Old Beauty," although a considerably more substantial piece of fiction, had been for several years complete but withheld from publication upon the advice of people who had Cather's best interests at heart. To read it is to validate John Chamberlain's unkind judgment of the previous decade, to the effect that good prose alone cannot provide the breath of life for a story that does not possess it otherwise. Cather's very last short work, "The Best Years," is a final attempt at depicting the Charles Cather family during Willa's girlhood and young adult years, but it fails entirely to create the necessary spark. All three of these stories were put between covers by Knopf soon after the author's death and published under the title *The Old Beauty and Others*. The collection, treated reverently by the critics, adds nothing of value to the Cather oeuvre. She seems to have understood better than her overly zealous publisher that her finest work—which was as expert, as glowing, as that of any other American writer—had long since been offered to the world. But the cream of the crop, that group of 10 or 12 stories in which everything coalesced, character, action, and theme combining with perfection, these are sufficient accomplishment. They by themselves place Cather within the first rank of American story writers, supporting her claim to permanence.

Chapter Seven
The Question of Cather Biography

You know how [Willa Cather] absolutely refused to let the world in on her personal life. She often said in her letters to people that everything the world was entitled to know was in her books.

Edith Lewis to Stephen Tennant, c. 1952

From the time of her young womanhood, Willa Cather courted fame, which for her meant the lasting renown that can be stimulated by fine written work and will arrive, soon or late, as the inevitable reward for a career dedicated to art. Her aim—the same of all writers, all artists, per-haps—was to defeat time by erecting an edifice that would endure the ravages of the years. Size did not matter: "Let him who will cavil of carv-ing cherry stones, it is the perfect thing, however small, that outlasts the ages wherein faulty epics are entombed without memorial."[1]

Guiding the Hand of Fate

By way of ensuring some such legacy for herself, Cather attempted so far as possible to manipulate the hand of fate, directing attention away from her person and toward what she considered to be the best of her writing. One might consider this: at any point from the mid-1920s onward, with her popularity among both readers and critics at a high-water mark, Cather might have chosen to issue a volume of "new" (hitherto-uncollected) stories from her backlog. She would have reaped a small fortune from their publication. Yet only a single volume of sto-ries appeared, *Obscure Destinies*, and its three stories were new ones. Even in preparing for the Library Edition of her collected works during the 1930s, Cather consigned to oblivion—a fate she felt was justly deserved—dozens of stories she had published in important magazines since the 1890s.

In an amazing Last Will and Testament, Cather continued her war against biography, forbidding direct quotations from any of her letters that might manage to survive her, while taking care also to place a ban on the publication of such letters. While she lived, Cather took measures aimed at ensuring that her letters would either be returned to her by their recipients for burning or be destroyed by the recipients themselves. Inevitably (and even while numerous letters did miraculously escape the slaughter), Cather's later biographers have been seriously hampered in their work by the loss of her letters to some of the correspondents closest to her, Isabelle McClung Hambourg being chief among them.

These are serious losses, crippling to biography, and Cather scholars have been forced to work as they might around the gaping holes left in the record by this destructive act, attempting all the while to place the best light possible on Cather's motivation, to believe that all of this havoc was worked in order to highlight the work, not the woman. One thinks inevitably of Emily Dickinson's words: "If fame belonged to me, I could not escape her—if she did not, the longest day would pass me on the chase."[2] But one might remember that Dickinson, even if not publishing while alive, did take care to leave her literary remains in nicely arranged shape for posterity to find. It was her sister, not the poet, who burned the letters Emily had received from correspondents.

The continuation, indeed the persistent growth, of Cather's fame has made the problem of her biography critical. Not only were her novels and stories grounded in autobiography (a fact made clear by the simplest of research as well as by her own admissions), but we live in a time when it is generally assumed that the personality as well as the outlined history of an artist will impinge meaningfully upon the work produced. Biography has never been more popular, more in demand. But Cather did whatever she could to de-emphasize her life story, to intermingle fiction with the facts concerning her life, to obscure the record, and to suppress biographical inquiry entirely whenever possible. This fact by itself has raised questions that both taunt and tantalize Cather's biographers. For *if* she sought to suppress the facts, *why* did she so earnestly wish to obliterate the record? Ultimately the question arises, What *was* that record, what *were* the facts?

From the beginning, Cather's biographers have had to grapple with a paucity of reliable data. Very little concerning Cather's life story ever became available while she was living, and what documents did appear were fragmentary and only quasi-reliable. The "facts" of her life always remained ambiguous at heart. Even Cather's age came into question after her death, she having given out as authentic the year 1876 rather than the actual date of 1873. In 1915, simultaneously with publishing *The Song of the Lark*, Houghton Mifflin printed a biographical pamphlet purporting to give the life history of Willa Cather, but it was learned, much later, that Cather herself wrote the account, and from that time it has not been easy for biographers to separate fact from fiction.

The first book devoted solely to Cather's life and writing did make an attempt at something approaching a comprehensive biographical sketch. That was René Rapin's *Willa Cather* (1930), commissioned by Robert W. McBride for his Modern American Authors series. Rapin of necessity depended upon what written sources were then available. One was the widely circulated interview given by Cather to Latrobe Carroll for the *Bookman* in May 1921, an interview that has since been shown to be loaded with inaccuracies. Rapin also used the somewhat more substantial chapter on Cather in Grant M. Overton's *The Women Who Make Our Novels* (1918), a chapter based largely on the Houghton Mifflin publicity pamphlet of 1915. Rapin also corresponded directly with Cather, hoping for help from the primary source, but Cather answered his inquiries with data that were not always factually correct. Clearly the time was too soon and the specifics too flawed to produce much of even passing value, but even so, Rapin best represents those few who dared attempt biography during the author's lifetime.

The "Knopf Pamplet" of 1928 was Rapin's third major source.[3] He and most other early biographers were driven to depend upon this 23-page publication, which began with a supposedly anonymous biographical sketch actually composed by Cather herself. Following it came a praising essay by an English critic and another by an American. Then came Cather's own, previously printed letter to *Commonweal* concerning *Death Comes for the Archbishop*, and the pamphlet closed with a much-abridged bibliography of Cather's writings. "When Willa Cather was eight years old," wrote the "author" of the biographical sketch, "her father took his family to Nebraska and bought a ranch near Red Cloud." Perhaps the word *ranch* had a more exciting ring to it than the more pedestrian *farm*, but in any case, it was cropland the Cathers settled on, temporarily. The error persisted in accounts of Cather's life for years, of course. "Farming was then a secondary matter," said the sketch, "and the most important occupation was the feeding of great herds of cattle driven up from Texas, and most of the great prairie country from the Missouri River to Denver was still open grazing land."[4] That is correct—up to a point. But the statement begs the question of whether Charles Cather's property was grazing land or cropland and does not specify whether or not the Cathers were engaged in feeding those Texas herds (they were not).

Concerning her years spent in Pittsburgh, years it appeared Cather would just as soon forget after having moved to the number-one city, New York, the Knopf Pamphlet insisted that Cather spent only the winters in the Steel City: "Every summer she went back to Nebraska and Colorado and Wyoming."[5] True again—up to a point. The pamphlet does not claim outright that Cather spent her entire summers away from Pittsburgh, although any reader might be pardoned for drawing such an inference from the ambiguous manner of the statement.

Residents of Cather's hometown, Red Cloud, have always been appealed to for what they could contribute to the record. A strange mid-1930s addition to the folklore surrounding her was the "Story by Willa Cather's Neighbors," which bore the subtitle "As Told to Elsie Goth" when it appeared in the university publication the *Nebraska Alumnus*. Both interesting and gossipy (and probably unreliable in toto), the "Story" reported that Cather's old neighbors in Nebraska could recall "the days when [Willa] deliberately refused to go to school, when she was planning to become a doctor of if not a doctor an undertaker, when she was one of America's first co-eds with bobbed hair, when by sheer will power and perseverance she cured herself of lameness," and that as a youngster living in the Catherton district she had "appointed herself postmistress for the community and rode twelve miles each day for the mail."[6] The legends that were being spawned here might be spurious at best, but the interest in the life story of "Nebraska's Own" world-famous author was surely genuine. Readers not only in Nebraska but in the wide world beyond were hungry to know more about Willa Cather.

During the early 1940s, the scholar Benjamin D. Hitz became seriously interested in probing Cather's life, and he hired Flora Bullock, who had been a classmate of Cather's at the university, to help with his research. Desirous of obtaining data on Cather's young womanhood, Hitz expressed his opinion that Rapin's biography was not worth much to him, containing almost no original material, most being taken from other sources—and there seemed mighty few of these that Hitz had been able to identify. One was the Latrobe Carroll article in the *Bookman*, another the Houghton Mifflin prospectus of 1915. He thought that the University of Nebraska should be a storehouse of information, and he wanted Bullock, who lived in Lincoln, to research the matter. Cather's sister Jessica was then a Lincoln resident as well, and she might be "approachable,"[7] Hitz thought. But he had much to learn about how closemouthed Cather's siblings could be—or, to state it another way, how faithful they could be to their big sister's insistence upon privacy.

The 1950s and the First Flowering of Biography

The lid of silence was not lifted until after Cather's death in 1947 and the approval by her literary executor and longtime companion, Edith Lewis, of Professor E. K. Brown of the University of Chicago as the author of a full-length biography. Brown had published articles on Cather and her work in scholarly journals since 1936, and at the time of Cather's death the two were in correspondence. Brown not only had at his disposal the many short fragments of biography that had appeared during the course of decades (whether he knew of Cather's role in writing them is another matter) but, much more important, had access to the record made available by Edith Lewis, who lived with Cather for 40 years, as well as the considerable files of Cather's publisher, Alfred A. Knopf, and many of Cather's letters that had escaped destruction.

Unfortunately, E. K. Brown died in 1951, his biography incomplete. But fortuitously, it was finished by Leon Edel, since become known as one of the nation's foremost biographers of literary figures. The Brown-Edel biography, providing far and away the most complete picture of Cather's life and work, upon its 1953 publication at once became the standard work in its field, to be relied upon by all scholars who followed.

During the same year Brown-Edel's *Willa Cather: A Critical Biography* appeared, Edith Lewis published her memoir *Willa Cather Living: A Personal Record*, which originally had been written as an assist to E. K. Brown. Based upon data picked up during Lewis's long association with Cather, supplemented by data gleaned from Cather's friends and her siblings, to whom Lewis had access, *Willa Cather Living* fills in any number of lacunae. It is far from being a perfect work, however. Not only does it necessarily repeat much of what was simultaneously appearing in Brown-Edel, but, significantly, it established Lewis's control over biographical facts, allowing into print only the data that Lewis chose to release, giving them the spin that best suited her purpose, and restricting access to those areas of the Cather-Lewis association Lewis felt must remain unprobed. The book makes a valuable record nevertheless.

Also in 1953 appeared *Willa Cather: A Memoir*, by Elizabeth Shepley Sergeant, a work produced independently of either Lewis or Brown-Edel and based upon Sergeant's close association with Cather since 1910. The chief source of the memoir, aside from Sergeant's personal recollections, which were considerable, was the scores of letters she had received from the novelist between 1910 and 1946. Their correspondence was particularly heavy during the decades between 1910 and 1930, years crucial to Cather's burgeoning career. The letters, many of them lengthy, crammed with detail and opinion, touch upon areas of Cather's experience not treated elsewhere (although silent, as might be expected in that historical context, on the question of sexual orientation). They are drawn on heavily and constitute, in fact, the outstanding aspect of Sergeant's memoir. A unique account by one who knew the novelist intimately, this is a work of permanent value.

The timing of publication allowed Sergeant to verify objective details such as dates against both Lewis and Brown-Edel. Sergeant also had the advantage of seeing three other important, if relatively minor, contributions to the initial burst of biographical interest in Cather. The first of these other works to go to press (1950) had been *These Too Were Here*, a slim memoir by Elizabeth Moorhead. As the work is devoted also to recollections of Pittsburgh-born Louise Homer, contralto with the Metropolitan Opera, the space allotted to Cather—less than 20 pages— seems minimal. Yet Moorhead provides a vivid picture of Pittsburgh in the 1905 era when, reading "Paul's Case" in *McClure's*, she determined to introduce herself to the author and thank her in person for writing it. Moorhead takes the reader inside the big McClung house at 1180 Murray Hill Avenue and provides a rare, firsthand view of Cather, her great friend Isabelle McClung, and the way in which life was carried on in that household. In later years, Moorhead corresponded on an occasional basis with Cather, and in her memoir she quotes at some length, apparently not having heard—or else choosing to disregard—the novelist's interdiction concerning her correspondence. But the student of Willa Cather is much the richer for it.

During 1950 also, from the University of Nebraska Press, there had arrived James R. Shively's slim but important volume *Writings from Willa Cather's Campus Years*, reprinting a smattering of Cather's early (1890–95) fiction, drama criticism, and poetry. But the chief contribution Shively makes is to biography, for he was the first to seriously question Cather's purported birthdate and make a systematic effort to establish the truth. He also corresponded with those of Cather's university classmates that he could reach. And because he reprinted their responses, the young Willa Cather is revealed firsthand through the impact she made upon her contemporaries.

The most substantial effort at depicting Cather's early life had followed in 1951. It was *The World of Willa Cather*, by that remarkable
woman Mildred R. Bennett, who, coming to live in Red Cloud, made
herself into an authority on the most prominent local celebrity. Her book
is a good corrective to pieces of gossip such as the 1930s Goth article in
the *Nebraska Alumnus*. Organizing her data on a topical basis rather than
moving according to any chronological pattern, Bennett made available
a wealth of information concerning Cather's early life, with an emphasis
upon the years in Red Cloud and Lincoln. More than 30 photographs,
most of them not previously published, documented the Virginia background and the Webster County girlhood. Bennett's list of acknowledg-
ments was testimony to the success of her efforts to canvass Webster
County for the reminiscences of those who knew Cather personally. And
in writing her book, Bennett had the advantage of working closely with
Cather's best and oldest Red Cloud friend, Carrie Miner Sherwood,
whose family had served as the model for the Harlings in *The Song of the
Lark*, Carrie being Frances Harling. Bennett's work endures as an
invaluable sourcebook for Cather scholars.

The 1980s and the Resurgence of Biography

The flowering of biographical studies in 1953 satisfied the needs of interested followers of Cather until, two decades later, Phyllis C. Robinson
published her biography *Willa: The Life of Willa Cather*. The informality
of the title signals Robinson's aim at the popular reader, for this volume
is without scholarly pretensions. Intended for leisurely reading, it is
based, Robinson says, on her wish to learn whatever she could about the
favorite author of her girlhood; "[she] stirred my heart and kindled my
imagination with tales of an America and a time I had never known."[7]
The manner in which Robinson set out to recapture her revered author
was to delve into her letters. Instinctively, that was the right direction to
head in, for the letters might reveal the real woman. To do this required
much traveling to libraries, travel Robinson combined with the de
rigueur pilgrimage to Webster County, Nebraska, the locale for so much
of Cather's fiction.

Robinson utilizes the Cather letters almost to the exclusion of available printed sources for biography. They are paraphrased in detail, and,
in fact, considerable portions of *Willa* are made up almost wholly of such
paraphrases, stitched together into paragraphs and pages. Because the
resultant story hews so very close to Cather's own words, this procedure

lends a sense of immediacy, and of authenticity, to the prose, the happy sense that as readers we are there, on the spot, at the moment, seeing through Cather's eyes, listening with her ears. It all makes Robinson's book highly readable, fast moving, and colorful.

But Cather's letters can be a trap for the unwary. They are the letters of a literary sophisticate, and it pays to read them with one's own sense of sophistication intact, to recall rather constantly Cather's penchant for embellishing the truth about herself, her habit at times even of falsifying the record. To rely, for biography, upon the surface story of these letters is to provide oneself with an endless array of colorful particularities. But it also means placing oneself at the mercy of Willa Cather, letter writer. For her, letters too often were just another form of creative writing. Turning them out at what, to judge from her handwriting, seems breakneck speed, she seems to have felt little obligation to hold strictly to verifiable fact, seems often out to impress or to entertain or even to tease her correspondent. Whether in fiction or in letters, Cather relished getting a rise out of her reader. And so, to accept the letters uncritically can be a costly mistake. And when one lets down his guard and allows his own subjectivity to enter into the transcriptions, some real potential for gaffes exists.

Neither of these booby traps is avoided entirely by Robinson, as an examination of specific passages of her book will demonstrate. As an example, we might consider her account (p. 173) of Cather's trip to Arizona during the late spring of 1912 and her residence with her brother Douglass in Winslow. This was, as it turned out, a crucial time for Cather, being her first real exposure to a section of the United States that almost at once assumed an important role in her fiction. Winslow was a small desert town on the Santa Fe Railroad, for which Douglass worked. It became a base point for trips to Flagstaff, Walnut Canyon, the Grand Canyon, Albuquerque, Santa Fe, Taos, and the small Indian villages of New Mexico, an exhilarating time for Cather as measured by the length, frequency, and intensity of the letters she wrote, chiefly to her new friend Elizabeth Shepley Sergeant.

It is the letters to Sergeant on which Robinson has relied when composing her own account of Cather's experience, an account that includes this group of sentences:

> Winslow depressed her terribly. She hated the sandstorm and the wind and the tin cans whirling about the streets. The people lived in flimsy, run-down shacks and while Douglass' house was more commodious than

most, there was no spot in it for her to work. The air of the place was off, she wrote to Elsie. The Mexicans were her only compensation, even though, with her Midwestern prejudice, she considered them an inferior lot. Nevertheless, they had good manners, at least they went their own way, and she liked the sound of their musical speech.[8]

Unfortunately, few of the particulars in this passage can be verified by Cather's letters to Sergeant, which I recently examined at the Pierpont Morgan Library. Despite the town's many inconveniences, Winslow did not depress Cather at all. She was, after all, a graduate of the Red Cloud school of experience, and the place held few surprises for her. But she was sure that Winslow *would* depress *Sergeant*, the relatively sheltered easterner, Bostonian, product of Bryn Mawr, who had considered accompanying Cather and still expressed a notion of joining her in the Southwest. Cather had experienced the hot winds that blew up from Kansas in July to shrivel the Nebraska corn crop in three days. But at the very first gust of windblown sand in Winslow, she could picture her friend's probable reaction. The panicked Sergeant would leap onto the earliest outgoing train, wearing only her nightdress if necessary. She wrote Sergeant to this effect, mincing no words.[9]

Cather never referred to the "casas" of Winslow as being in run-down condition, nor did she write of tin cans whirling in the streets (they *were* strewn among the ground litter, however). And as for the notion of Cather having a "Midwestern prejudice" against Mexicans, that accusation flies in the face of everything we know about her, seems wholly the dream child of Robinson, and is confounded by the Sergeant letters themselves, which say outright that Cather, when her housemates were away, might have perished of loneliness but for the Mexicans of Winslow who, even though relegated to the wrong side of the tracks by the Anglo population, kept a more charming neighborhood, spoke a lovelier tongue, and exhibited impeccable manners.[10]

To be sure, the Cather letters are to be read at one's own risk. James Woodress's *Willa Cather: Her Life and Art* (1970) was among the best of the general introductions to Cather, books generally combining biography with criticism. He had done a good deal of original research in primary sources not available to E. K. Brown but had not intended using these data in a straight biography until after the untimely death of Bernice Slote in 1983. Slote, a professor of English at the University of Nebraska and probably the foremost Cather scholar of her time, had amassed a great deal of data intended for use in attempting the definitive biography. These plans disrupted, Woodress changed his mind, deciding after all to take up the biography as a project. Using his own materials, and those gathered by Slote, augmented by new research, he produced in 1987 his magnum opus, *Willa Cather: A Literary Life*. Woodress discovered no reason to alter his previous conception of Cather as a person or his judgments concerning her novels, finding "no skeletons in the closet or sensational data to titillate the reader." But there were new details by the hundreds—by the thousands, really—to be added to the record. By no means *biographie démeublé*, the result of Woodress's efforts is a huge compendium of just about everything to be known about Cather up to the time of writing. In its considerable heft—the volume falls just shy of 600 pages, compared with the 288 of the 1970 version—and in its completeness as well, the new *Willa Cather* had as one of its unspoken aims to be so far as possible a day-by-day account. In that way it hews to one of the more popular modern formats for biography, following the pattern set by tomes such as Mark Shorer's *Sinclair Lewis: An American Life* (1961; 876 pp.), W. A. Swanberg's *Dreiser* (1965; 614 pp.), and Carlos Baker's *Ernest Hemingway: A Life Story* (1969; 697 pp.). In Woodress the interested reader will find most everything he wants or needs to know; the book serves as a vast, reliable, and well-written reference work and undoubtedly will continue to serve satisfactorily in that capacity for a good many years.

Much of what is new in Woodress comes from Cather's personal and business correspondence. Woodress himself estimates that something like 1,500 Cather letters survive, most of these—notable exceptions being Cather's letters to members of her family—now on deposit in libraries whose locations range from Maine to California. There seems no reason to doubt that Woodress has read each of them. Other scholars who also have read these letters, or portions of them, recognize that Woodress has used them with an unfettered sense of freedom, closely paraphrasing in order to flesh out the Cather story with particulars. They are reminded at the same time of how much of the record must still be missing—lost to us forever, probably, although perhaps recoverable in part—as a result of Cather's (and Edith Lewis's) campaign to suppress/destroy all of the novelist's personal papers. An apparent justification might be found in a paraphrase of Cather's remark on one her own favorites among her predecessors, Edgar Allan Poe: "The woman is nothing, her work everything." Modern readers may disagree.

When Woodress deviates from the diarylike aspect of the biography, it usually is to take up a discrete topic for development as a set piece. He does, for instance, a very nice job of defending Cather against the charge of anti-Semitism, tracing carefully through her published works to establish that her fiction overall maintains what might be called a realistic balance between the number of Jewish characters who indulge in skullduggery and the number who are held up as praiseworthy members of the human family. Woodress's critical estimates of the various novels form another series of essays, his judgments always being judicious, his opinions based on solid thinking. Comparing Cather's work with that of some of her contemporaries, Woodress imagines the reader as a swimmer who, if he dives into Sinclair Lewis, for example, is in danger of banging his head on the bottom; if he dives into Thomas Wolfe, he will be struck, as by a submerged rock, by the painful disparity between the man's exuberant prose and the power of his mind. But the swimmer in Cather's writing "can dive as deep as he wishes and stay down as long as he can." While she was not a writer of "intellectual novels," her works contain substance aplenty; they nourish the mind and the emotions alike.[11]

Woodress works a new vein in considering Cather's relationships with her publishers, especially on the central event in that record, her defection in 1921 from Boston and Houghton Mifflin to New York and Alfred Knopf. (Her admiring relationship with Knopf, incidentally, constitutes convincing vindication of any charge that Cather was anti-Semitic.) Cather in 1940 wrote her own account of the manner in which the changeover occurred, making it all sound quite low-key, spontaneous, and brought about almost as if by happenstance or fortunate accident. This story Woodress does not hesitate to label a pure instance of the "autobiographical fiction" in which Cather had indulged periodically all through her adult years. In actuality, Cather had for some time—a number of years—been dissatisfied with the manner in which Houghton Mifflin published and advertised her books. She felt that the company did a poor job of distributing copies (as, for instance, to the magazines most likely to come up with good reviews) and that it did not seem to care about keeping a satisfactory backlog of copies in stock. Ferris Greenslet of Houghton Mifflin corresponded with Cather at some length concerning her complaints, but despite his patient explanations and denials, and the length of his service as her editor, he was unable to dissuade her from abandoning his firm for a New York–based publisher. As for Knopf, he had wooed Cather over a period of many months. Having decided that her long-term reputation was headed for the stars, he persuaded her that he was just the man to help her soar above the literary horizon.

Willa Cather: A Literary Life is in most respects an uncontroversial book, but on the issue of sexual politics Woodress displays his own conservatism by declining to leap onto the lesbian bandwagon that was already rolling while his biography was being written—a trend he recognizes. By 1982 Sharon O'Brien had published her interpretation of Cather's story "The Burglar's Christmas" (see the following discussion) as reflecting a problem of sexual identity and had stated as well her opinion that Jim Burden in *My Ántonia* was essentially a mask used to perpetuate and sanction limiting male views of women. Woodress was aware of O'Brien's views and those of other feminists, but he refused to bite on what must have been a real temptation to capitalize on a sensational theory in a book that was bound to be influential in the literary world. Woodress readily admits that, as an adult, Cather subscribed to a "bias against romantic love" and that a great failing in her work is her inability to portray heterosexual love convincingly. But he also refers to Cather as a "celibate" author, which would suggest nonparticipation in any form of active lesbianism.[12] The issue comes to a head, of course, over the issue of Cather's relationship with Isabelle McClung, and Woodress, after considering the evidence here and on other sexually related aspects of Cather's life, attempts to have it both ways. If to be called lesbian requires indulgence in a physical relationship, then Cather was not a lesbian, for "there is no external evidence to support" such a view. But if the term *lesbian* refers to a woman's primary emotional bonds being with other women, "then Cather was most certainly a lesbian." In the end, he concludes, it is "impossible to say" which of these definitions represents truth, and says that critics who use the lesbian label indulge in "inference, not fact."[13]

Here Woodress seems to be trapped in something of an evolving conflict of opinions (trapped as well, perhaps, by his own age, gender, and background), the eventual answer to which possibly lies in evidence not yet producible. This is not a large failing in the Woodress biography, but it is the single important point on which controversy is likely to persist in a volume that is a major contribution to Cather studies.

Published in the same year as Woodress's "official" biography was *Willa Cather: The Emerging Voice*, by Sharon O'Brien. It has been, by all odds, the most challenging volume on Cather to appear. Although O'Brien says that she did not at the outset expect to deal with Cather as a lesbian writer, once she had read the handful of letters that survive from the author's correspondence with Louise Pound, she changed her mind. Pound had been Cather's classmate at the University of Nebraska, had visited Cather in Red Cloud during the 1890s, and Cather had written explicitly that she had fallen in love with her. These letters persuaded O'Brien that the label "lesbian" named Cather's self-definition precisely and that there was no point in proceeding with her biography unless she were willing to consider the impact on Cather's creativity of her great need both to hide and to disclose her experience of desire.

Once the lesbian label is brought out into the open, all the facts of Cather's life take on new significance. O'Brien sees the Cather childhood as torn psychologically by a gender struggle that became more pronounced during adolescence. Identifying "creativity" with masculinity—which appeared to be the world's opinion—and finding herself, as female, outside the pale, Cather made her well-known attempts to "switch sexes" through names, clothing, and activities, adopting male-assigned roles whenever possible. It was a long struggle to reach a point whereby being female did not severely limit her "universality" as a writer (and some might argue that Cather never did quite reach that goal).

O'Brien locates at least a part of Cather's problem in her confusion regarding her relationship with her mother. That Willa was the oldest of seven children was an important factor in establishing her psychological makeup. It meant, for one thing, that she observed her mother as the perennial producer of a series of younger rivals for maternal attention and affection. What Willa knew as a girl growing up in this family was that her mother took special pains to adorn herself for men (the holders of the real power in the world). Mary Virginia Boak Cather did rule within the walls of her house, but she wielded no real power in the larger society beyond her property line—where Willa hoped to achieve and make a name for herself. To do that, she would need to make herself into the facsimile of a man.

O'Brien explains the significance of the gender dilemma as a cause for Cather's extraordinarily long apprenticeship, pointing to it in regard to Cather's "conflict-ridden" endeavor of producing a novel when she was otherwise convinced that novel writing was something properly done by men. It seemed audacious, indeed dangerous, for her to enter this male preserve, leaving behind the province of the short story, the sketch, especially the local-color piece, those writings considered appropriate for a woman who aspired to write. That helps to explain why Cather was nearly 40 years old before she produced a novel, and that when she did, it had a male at the center of its story and was written in imitation of the most honored and influential male writer of her day, Henry James. Cather's statement to Louise Imogen Guiney, written as late as 1911, is cited tellingly. Given the choice between reading a novel written by a man and one written by a woman, Cather would choose that by the male: "I prefer to take no chances when I read."[14]

The O'Brien thesis leads directly to exciting new interpretations of Cather stories, including some that previously were viewed as mere trifles. "The Burglar's Christmas" tells the rather fanciful story of a young man, long separated from his family, who enters a mansion clandestinely and burglarizes the wife's bedroom, where her jewels and other precious family objects are kept. There he discovers his own baby's mug, and then he encounters his own mother. O'Brien ties this story's psychological underpinnings to the themes of major fiction to come, wherein so often the search for a comforting maternal figure is featured. "The Burglar's Christmas" illuminates something of the costs as well as the benefits involved in returning to the mother. While the thief (interestingly, named William and Willie, the identical boy-names Willa Cather had adopted for herself as a girl) does gain desirable things such as food, contentment, and maternal love from the reunion with his mother, he loses his autonomy and his separate identity. He slides, writes O'Brien, "into a state of proverbial infantile bliss which is remarkably similar to death."[15]

The Future of Cather Biography

Difficult (or impossible) as it might be to predict what is to come, at this writing there seems little reason to doubt that Sharon O'Brien has caught the wave of the future as it concerns Cather biography. Just as it would make no sense for a future biographer to ignore the profit to be gained from the encyclopedic contribution of Woodress, it seems equally clear that from this time no life study of the novelist can be taken seriously if it fails to give due consideration to the O'Brien thesis. Hermione Lee's *Willa Cather: Double Lives* (1989), at this moment the major post-Woodress/O'Brien contribution, takes cognizance of both of these landmark books. Although she describes her approach to Cather as decidedly "not a biographical tour,"[16] Lee does rely heavily upon an interpretation of Cather biography as an aid to explaining her understanding of the intricate braiding together of Cather's life facts with her fictional stories.

The sheer magnitude of Woodress, combined with its tone of adulation, influences Lee to credit it with representing a climactic point in the "Cather hagiography" she identifies as centering in Lincoln, Nebraska. Undoubtedly, Woodress has served Lee as a valuable resource, but just as clearly O'Brien is more intriguing for her. She cites it as an instance of "inspired new readings"[17] of Cather, and her specific citations from it far outweigh those from Woodress. The references made to Cather's sexual proclivities in pre-O'Brien studies are here branded timid and inexplicit, "squeamish" finally being the term Lee most prefers. But blindly to appropriate Cather into the cause of radical feminism seems to Lee most wrongheaded: "To account for Cather's fiction by reading it as an encoding of covert, even guilty, sexuality, is, I think, patronizing and narrow. It assumes that the work is written only in order to express homosexual feeling in disguise; it makes her out to be a coward (which was certainly not one of her failings); and it assumes that 'openness' would have been preferable [but] Cather is diminished by being enlisted into a cause. She was a writer who worked, at her best, through induction, suppression and suggestion, and through a refusal to be enlisted."[18]

As we might expect from her highly suggestive subtitle, Lee's study of Cather is deeply grounded in psychology and even in Cather's own near admission that she might have a split personality. Lee makes hay of the commonplace observation that in Cather events and people often pull two ways. Lee, of course, relates this phenomenon to the inner struggles that sometimes made a battlefield of Cather's personal and professional lives and that found release in her writing. Cather's work, in fact, derives its chief appeal from the tensions created by its—and her—contrary positions: "She is pulled between the natural and the artificial, the native and the European. She is a democrat and an elitist. She relishes troll-like energy and primitivism as much as delicacy and culture. She is equally interested in renunciation and possessiveness, in impersonality and obsession. Her fictions are all split selves and doubles."[19] All of Cather's works—her career in writing itself—are related, says Lee, to the insecurities that underlie the Cather personality and have their roots in her biography. There were her worries, as eldest child, over her family's financial problems during the 1890s; the struggles of her Pittsburgh years also left their mark. She regularly saved money from her wages and sent it home to help out, and even at age 39 she got the jitters just to think of leaving her "safe job" at *McClure's* for the scary prospect of freelancing as a novelist. Cather's lack of confidence reveals itself even (or perhaps most dramatically) in what might otherwise be trivialities; to advance her date of birth for *Who's Who*, as an example, was "a deception [that] suggests considerable anxiety about her progress."[20]

Because of Lee's dual emphasis on biography and criticism, with Lee during Cather's middle years consciously turning away "from what happens in her life to what happens in her language,"[21] I will reserve for chapter 8 Lee's notions of the ways in which Cather's anxieties are reflected in the writing. But *Willa Cather: Double Lives* seems to be rather representative of what we might expect to see in the future, less a repetition of Woodress-style full-blooded biographies than a series of illuminating interpretive studies to which the facts of Cather's life are basic but not, finally, their reason for existence.

Chapter Eight

From Many Minds: Cather Scholarship

The portrait of a great artist, as it finally emerges, must come, I think, from many sources and from many minds.

Edith Lewis, 1953

At her death in 1947, Cather left uncollected an immense amount of writing, totaling in the aggregate many times that of the stories and novels upon which her fame then rested. For the first quarter-century after she died, a major task in Cather studies was to locate, edit, and publish these fugitive pieces: stories, essays, interviews, criticism, and reportage. Cather herself would probably have been content to leave 99 percent of her uncollected writings to moulder in the files of the newspapers and magazines that were their first publishers. For Cather, these works were ephemeral, written for specific occasions and not fit to be allowed the light of day more than once before being cast into darkness. But as more than one devotee has remarked, if we are to know Willa Cather and the road she traveled, then we must know not merely where that road took her but where her journey began.

Bringing in the Sheaves: Posthumous Volumes

Cather's posthumous publications got under way almost at once with Alfred A. Knopf's issuance in 1948 of her trio of final stories, *The Old Beauty and Others*, followed the next year by *Willa Cather on Writing*, a collection of critical statements notable for preserving her most famous essay, "The Novel Démeublé." The decade that followed was one of great activity, bringing James Shively's book of writings from Cather's college years, George N. Kates's edition of the travel letters Cather had written from Europe to the *Nebraska State Journal* in 1902, and Mildred R. Bennett's edition of 19 apprentice stories published between 1892 and 1900.

These, combined with the biographical works issued in 1953, gave Cather scholars much to consider; but during the 1950s the trickle of publications swelled to a flood, as scholars trained in professional methods turned up more new works than anyone knew had existed, including journalism—largely book, theatrical, and musical reviews—written on assignment while Cather was a college student. Somewhat amazingly, as it turned out, between 1890 and 1895 she had published considerably more in this vein than in all of her later novels combined. The continuing investigation into the files of old magazines, many of them extinct by now and difficult to come by, had by 1965 yielded what apparently was Cather's full oeuvre so far as short stories were concerned, and Virginia Faulkner of the University of Nebraska published the earliest of these under the title *Willa Cather's Collected Short Fiction, 1892–1912*. During the following year, Faulkner's colleague at Nebraska, Bernice Slote, edited a thick volume of Cather's cultural statements, *The Kingdom of Art*. And the next decade opened with publication of the much-anticipated two-volume compilation of Cather's early newspaper articles and reviews, *The World and the Parish*, edited by William M. Curtin.

In editing *Uncle Valentine and Other Stories* (1972), the short fiction written by Cather between 1915 and 1929 but never collected, Slote completed the work begun by Faulkner. This meant that nearly everything written by Willa Cather was—for the first time—available to scholars wishing to consider Cather's work in toto. The job was completed, as planned, before the date of the Centennial Festival organized by Slote and Robert E. Knoll, "The Art of Willa Cather: An International Seminar." Held in Lincoln in October 1973, the Seminar drew together 85 prominent scholars representing seven nations, as well as Cather-connected notables from the literary world such as Eudora Welty, Leon Edel, and Alfred A. Knopf.

Since 1975 the issuance of posthumous volumes has slowed but not ceased entirely, for in 1986 L. Brent Bohlke published his collection of interviews, speeches, and a handful of letters that had been published during Cather's lifetime: *Willa Cather in Person*. Bohlke joins the earlier Cather items to make more complete the set of valuable tools without which Cather scholarship would surely have lagged.

Catherland: The Transformation of Red Cloud

Paralleling the growth of Cather studies—largely the work of universities, libraries, and scholars—has been the growth of the Willa Cather Pioneer Memorial (WCPM), established in March 1955 in Red Cloud, Nebraska.[1] Aiding its guiding spirit, Mildred R. Bennett, were a group of Cather friends and relatives, educators, and local businesspeople. The aims of the WCPM were (and are) (1) to secure suitable housing for a collection of art, literature, and history relating to Cather and her times; (2) to identify and restore local places made famous by Cather; (3) to memorialize Cather through art and literary scholarships (amended in 1975 to include the encouragement and assistance of Cather scholarship generally); and (4) to perpetuate an interest in Cather on a worldwide basis.

Among the first donations to come to the WCPM were the books, letters, and artifacts collected by Cather's longtime local friend and correspondent Carrie Miner Sherwood and given to the WCPM in 1956. The gift included some 200 Cather letters as well as that copy of *O Pioneers!* in which Cather had written the much-quoted inscription saying that with this book she had finally landed a hit in her "home pasture." The Sherwood collection was placed on display on the second floor of Red Cloud's State Theatre Building, which was where the WCPM then housed the beginnings of its museum. At that same time, the emblem of the organization was selected: a representation of the plow silhouetted against the sun, from *My Ántonia*; it has been used as a logo ever since.

In 1957 the first issue of the *WCPM Newsletter*, a mimeographed sheet, hand-stamped, went out to 100 members and friends. The newsletter has continued to be published, at first on a semiannual basis and later as a quarterly, growing in size and importance. Today it serves as a major conduit not only for news concerning Willa Cather but for the publication of scholarly articles by many of the leading Cather scholars as well as newcomers to the field. Also, in 1955, student groups began to visit the museum on organized tours. Within three years these school groups were being bused on a 65-mile tour of "Cather Country" to visit the Divide and a variety of home and town sites used in Cather's fiction, places such as the Cather homes in the "Catherland" area and in Bladen, as well as the Pavelka farm (where Jim Burden first met Ántonia's children). In Red Cloud, the obvious need for a secure and permanent home for the WCPM and its burgeoning collection was satisfied by the purchase in 1959 of the tall, narrow, brick-and-stone bank building erected in 1889 by Silas Garber, prototype of Captain Forrester in *A Lost Lady*. The most imposing structure on Webster Street, the bank building had been used as Red Cloud City Hall for a time and still contained its solid, walk-in, brick-and-iron vault, the ideal (and picturesque) spot to press into service as storage for the letters, manuscripts, books, photographs, and other precious Cather mementos that were fast accumulating.

Using grants from the J. M. McDonald and Eugene C. Eppley foundations, the WCPM was able to restore the Garber Building in time for an official opening in May 1962. The first pair of visitors to enter were Cather's sisters, Elsie and Jessica. The new museum was air-conditioned through the generosity of R. S. Shannons, Mrs. Shannon being Cather's niece Margaret, daughter of her brother Roscoe. With the purchase of Cather's childhood home, the WCPM took a major step toward an ideal: acquisition of all local landmarks of signal importance to Cather's life and fiction. Great strides have been made toward realizing that ideal, and the effort continues.

In 1964 an official marker, the metal silhouette of an iron walking-plow, was set atop a concrete pedestal eight miles north of Red Cloud, alerting visitors and travelers that they were approaching what the WCPM was by now referring to as Catherland. The governor, Frank B. Morrison, presided at the dedication. Those plow markers began to proliferate after 1965 when the Nebraska State Legislature officially proclaimed that the term Catherland might be applied to the western half of Webster County. In Red Cloud, other structures joined those already owned by the WCPM: in 1965 the old Burlington Railroad depot, a mile south of town, to which the young Willa Cather walked with her friends to watch wide-eyed as traveling theatrical troupes unloaded their baggage and caught the coach into town, and in 1968 the tiny Catholic church of St. Juliana Falconieri, built in 1883, the year the Cathers arrived from Virginia, and the church in which "my Ántonia" (Annie Sadilek) was married to John Pavelka. In 1970 the Nebraska diocese of the Episcopal church deeded to the WCPM Grace Episcopal Church, whose parish Cather belonged to after her conversion in 1922; Cather's donations of stained-glass windows memorialize her parents, Charles and Virginia Cather.

South of Red Cloud, almost touching the Kansas border, lay a rare, untouched plot of native grassland. In 1974 this 610-acre tract became the Willa Cather Memorial Prairie, to remain forever wild, a reminder of the way that much of Webster County used to be when Cather moved there in 1883, its several kinds of grass and its plethora of wildflowers changing with the seasons. In Red Cloud itself, the most recent acquisition has been the brick business block on Webster Street, whose second story housed the Opera House, where in 1890 16-year-old Willa Cather delivered her high school commencement address in defense of scientific experimentation. Today the Cather sites are operated by the state of Nebraska, which has located a branch of the state historical society in the Garber Building, the old Farmers' and Merchants' Bank (the WCPM having moved three doors to the south).

The notion of holding an annual conference centered on Cather and her works bore fruit for the first time in 1955, and since then a conference has been sponsored every spring, the topic usually focusing upon a single Cather title. In addition, the WCPM sponsors national and international seminars that are popular gathering places not only for scholars but for everyday readers who appreciate Cather. The most recent of these, "The Fifth International Cather Seminar," was conducted 19–26 June 1993 on the campus of Hastings College in Hastings, Nebraska, north of Red Cloud. The seminar enrolled some 200 participants from the United States and abroad, some participants traveling from as far as Japan and India. Under the supervision of Patricia Phillips of the WCPM, the seminar staff was composed of Cather scholars Elizabeth Ammons, Marilyn Arnold, Bruce Baker, John J. Murphy, Ann Romines, and Susan Rosowski (who served as director). In addition, Terence Martin, Merrill Maguire Skaggs, and Cynthia Griffin Wolff were lecturers, and James Woodress the honored guest of the seminar. The seminar theme, "After the World Broke in Two," focused attention on Cather's post-1922 writing, and during the eight days of the seminar there was time for discussion of everything from *A Lost Lady* (1923) to "The Best Years" (1948), supplemented by leisurely bus tours of Red Cloud and the rural Catherland area. A spectacular prairie sunset with a red fireball sun touching the horizon had participants half expecting to see the silhouette of a walking-plow blaze against the fiery sky.

Harvest: Cather Studies at Maturity

During the past four decades, Willa Cather's life and works have provided the inspiration for any number of fine books. Several of these—biographical studies—have furnished the substance for chapter 7, and other outstanding contributions should be mentioned. *Willa Cather's Gift of Sympathy* (1962), by Edward A. and Lillian D. Bloom, comes to mind at once, as does Richard Giannone's *Music in Willa Cather's Fiction* (1968), which set a standard for studies of particular interests or themes that are important throughout the span of Cather's fiction. In a class all by itself is *Willa Cather's Imagination* (1975), whose author, David Stouck, has always had original ideas concerning Cather and invariably expresses them with economy and stylistic grace. Susan Rosowski, herself among the premier Cather scholars of our day, in 1986 expressed her conviction that Cather criticism had "reached impressive proportions in both quantity and quality."[2] I agree wholeheartedly with this judgment. But it is only within the past decade that book-length works by lifelong Cather scholars have emerged from the presses with a steady profusion that clearly signals a high-water mark. I consider seven of these books as I conclude this revision of my own general study of Cather, first published in 1975. These books, all issued between 1984 and 1992, make up the list of contributions that merit the very highest consideration by readers of Willa Cather. The listing is in chronological order of publication.

Ever since *The Troll Garden* first appeared in 1905, Cather has been recognized as the author of superb short stories and for decades has been represented in anthologies along with other masters of that genre, usually by "Paul's Case" or "Neighbour Rosicky." Among recent discrete treatments of the briefer works, the finest is perhaps Marilyn Arnold's book *Willa Cather's Short Fiction* (1984).

Arnold takes a chronological approach, beginning with Cather's first, sometimes awkward, clearly apprentice tales and concluding with her final story. Even so, Arnold takes pains not to mislead a reader into assuming that the time arrangement is employed because the stories in any way "chart a step-by-step pattern of artistic growth throughout a lifetime of writing."[3] Nothing could be further from the truth. Rather, Arnold recognizes that Cather's early stories display the products of a young and rapidly developing writer (by the time of *The Troll Garden*, Arnold points out, Cather was capable of her finest work), just as her last efforts are clearly those of a practiced and polished author. Between these two extremes, over time, occur a broad range of excellences and mediocrities. What is important about the short fiction, collectively, is that it functions somewhat as bricks and mortar, as substance and bonding agents, holding the whole of Cather's work together and providing it with continuity. For one thing, as Arnold points out, the stories sometimes provide the first working out of materials later treated in the novel format.

Arnold is excellent in relating individual story to individual story and showing the manner in which typical Cather characters, once employed, tend to reappear, and the ways in which they function as various types of narrators. In presenting individual stories, Arnold can be astute. Her understanding of the tensions illustrated in the early story "Behind the

Singer Tower," for instance, is keen. The setting in the metropolis, with its sprouting skyscrapers, is reflected in an emphasis upon "harsh, vertical lines." By way of contrast, the setting of "The Bohemian Girl," published the same year (1912), is dominated by lines that are long and horizontal. The one story, says Arnold, "is the essence of activity and bustle," whereas the other is "the essence of everlasting sameness and quietude. Nils and Clara [of "The Bohemian Girl"] feel the pull of both worlds, as Willa Cather did, for each world answers one side of their inner nature."[4]

Arnold is one of the relatively few scholars who have had the courage to label Cather's final story, "The Best Years," as an outright failure. Although defensive of the story regarding the charge of sentimentality, Arnold is refreshingly explicit concerning its weaknesses: "Perhaps partly because it has no plot in the usual sense, and because it acknowledges almost none of the tensions between individual and group lives that [are vital to fiction], 'The Best Years' at times seems more like a collection of artistically rendered memories and feelings about a place and its people than like a short story."[5] The volume is comprehensive, offering the reader just about everything he might ever want to know about the shorter fiction.

From an enviable position of leadership among Cather scholars of the 1980s, Susan J. Rosowski, in her study *The Voyage Perilous: Willa Cather's Romanticism* (1986), interprets Cather's fiction as falling neatly within the romantic mode. The definition she applies in explaining romanticism stresses the use of the creative, synthesizing imagination as a means of transforming and imparting meaning to an alien or meaningless material world, thus tying Cather to the literary movement that since the late eighteenth century has reacted against the dehumanizing implications contained in the strictly scientific worldview.

In this sense, Rosowski's thesis militates against those critics who would interpret Cather's fiction—especially her later novels—as evidence of no more than a sad retreat to a more idyllic past; rather, the fiction "demonstrates a response to change,"[6] maintains Rosowski. Each novel, in its turn, is seen as exemplifying a phase or aspect of the romantic. *Alexander's Bridge* becomes "an allegory"[7] about the romantic imagination in its most primitive form, energy flowing between the spiritual world and the physical one; *A Lost Lady* stands as "a carefully modulated romantic prose poem"[8] much in the manner of an ode by Keats; and *The Professor's House* offers "a romantic version of the Fall"[9] in which Godfrey St. Peter has suffered a lapse from creative imagination to reason and is searching for redemption. In *A Lost Lady* Neil Herbert invites inevitable disappointment because he seeks permanence in a world characterized by continual change; and Myra Henshaw of *My Mortal Enemy* is like him, a sentimental romanticist who expects from life and her husband considerably more than it is possible for either to deliver.

Rosowski is an expert on Cather's life (when she says that Thea Kronborg's hometown, "Moonstone, Colorado, *is* Red Cloud, Nebraska," reproduced in fiction so precisely that one could map the stores, churches, houses, and streets,[10] you can be certain that the italicized *is* has not been dropped in hapazardly), and Rosowski, like most seasoned Cather scholars, draws upon the life whenever possible to support her interpretations and fasten down her concepts. But she very wisely resists the temptation to produce psychobiography. Instead, the life is used continually but sparingly and always with telling effect, as when, perceiving the roots of *Sapphira and the Slave Girl* as tapping into America's blindness, gullibility, and inaction as its response to the rise during the 1930s of world-threatening dictators such as Stalin, Hitler, and Mussolini, Rosowski calls Cather's final novel her most directly political piece of writing. The central tension in *Sapphira* is defined as "the inaction of characters against the increasingly disturbing and, finally, evil action of a powerful central figure."[11] In such remarks Rosowski's defining trait of the romantic, the response to change, is made concrete.

A high point of Rosowski's study is her chapter on *The Song of the Lark*, a book that was for Cather what *The Prelude* was for Wordsworth or *Sartor Resartus* for Carlyle: an investigation of the self as the source of value in an otherwise meaningless world. Here Rosowski's knowledge of the Cather biography is used with telling effect, for "Thea Kronborg is Willa Cather in essentials,"[12] even though the opera singer Olive Fremstad served as the ostensible model for the story's heroine. Wordsworth and Carlyle are invoked as artist models for Willa-Thea, both having needed to work their way through much the same dilemma of a "superior individual pitted against a common world."[13]

The Song of the Lark is presented as a "romantic Künstlerroman"[14] that characterizes the growth of an artist's mind and art. Thea must work her way out of the depressing muddle her life seems in Chicago, and, like Wordsworth returning to nature or Carlyle, via his Professor Teufelsdröckh, responding to the "Everlasting Yea," she must come to see life more clearly, more positively. This is the function of Thea's weeks spent in Panther Canyon, constituting a rebirth that alters her response to life, causes her to understand at last what the terms *art* and *artist* truly signify, and then allows her to realize her destiny as a singer. It is in *Lark* that Cather first "came to terms with her heritage";[15] and Rosowski's is the most thoroughly satisfying explication of the novel that I know.

The most original contribution of *The Voyage Perilous* comes in its final chapters, which are devoted to Cather's development of the Gothic strand of romanticism. That the "dark counterforce to optimistic romanticism"[16] had been present from the beginning as an element in Cather's writing is persuasively documented in references to early efforts such as "The Fear That Walks by Noonday," "The Affair at Grover Station," and "The Profile," all of which show evidence of Gothic elements such as dark reversals and doubling, use of grotesques, reliance on the uncanny, and emphasis upon emotions like horror and fear. Cather's use of the Gothic is traced story by story, novel by novel, arriving eventually at Rosowski's pair of prime examples, *Lucy Gayheart* and *Sapphira and the Slave Girl*. Clement Sebastian, the musician with whom Lucy Gayheart is infatuated, is here interpreted as a "Gothic Byronic hero," sophisticated on the surface, but beneath this facade prepared to renounce life, a jaded pessimist who clings to Lucy desperately to feed off her air of unspoiled youth. As the novel proceeds, it comes to resemble "nothing so much as *Dracula*, Bram Stoker's 1892 tale of dark possession and threatening sexuality,"[17] says Rosowski, *Dracula* retold from a woman's point of view. This unusual reading of Cather's novel is a fascinating, step-by-step series of parallels with Stoker's tale of the vampire, a reading that may be resisted even while one is being persuaded of its legitimacy. New light is shed on Lucy, on Sebastian, and on Harry Gordon, who emerges here as a life force who would draw Lucy *into* the world rather than, like Sebastian, out of it. Even Lucy's drowning when she breaks through the ice on the Platte and her skate catches on a submerged tree—a death that so many have called arbitrary or meaningless—is here shown to be symbolically appropriate, and perhaps inevitable, because "the major emotion of the book is of being 'gripped from underneath' by a submerged feeling of emptiness, in response to which characters cling briefly to something before they are pulled under."[18]

This is revisionist criticism at its most compelling, and Rosowski's continuation in the same vein regarding *Sapphira and the Slave Girl* brings her fine book to a resounding close.

John J. Murphy has long been prominent in Cather studies as the author of scores of articles and the author/editor of books such as *Critical Essays on Willa Cather* (1984). But his outstanding contribution to date is

probably *"My Ántonia": The Road Home*, (1989), a book-length study of
the novel Murphy quite rightly considers to be Cather's finest and most
consistently appealing work of fiction.

The critical reception to *My Ántonia* from the day of its publication in
1918 to the 1980s includes views expressed by a galaxy of writers who
range from H. L. Mencken and Henry W. Boynton to Blanche Gelfant
and Deborah Lambert. Murphy's review of this commentary demonstrates the many interpretations that have been offered, extending from
analyses of the novel as excelling in its portraiture of the western setting
and in the characterization of Ántonia herself to the novel's treatment of
sexuality and, indeed, to the question of Cather's own sexual orientation.

The bulk of Murphy's pages are devoted to an exhaustive reading and
textual commentary. Of special note are the important links Murphy
points out between the verbal artistry of *My Ántonia* and the canvases of
nineteenth-century painters of peasant life, such as Jean-François Millet
and Jules Breton of the Barbizon school, as well as affinities with
American landscape painters with impressionistic tendencies.
Particularly perceptive is the examination of links with luminist painters
such as Archer B. Durand, John E. Kensett, and Martin Johnson Heade.
For Murphy, the "supreme luminist scene"[19] in Cather's novel is her
famous image of a plow silhouetted in black against the molten red of a
setting sun.

Except for a tendency to accept Jim Burden rather than Ántonia as
the novel's chief character (would the book be anything at all lacking
Ántonia?) and to push too hard on the importance of the several
Virgilian and biblical allusions, Murphy's is the finest as well as the most
extensive study of *My Ántonia* that we have. It is to Murphy's credit that
he not only recognizes the biographical contribution of Sharon O'Brien
in exploring Cather's lesbianism but summarizes her theories sympa-
thetically and at some length. Although he warns that O'Brien's thesis
"remains speculative among cautious scholars,"[20] Murphy is successful in
suggesting that perhaps he is not too cautious himself to be accepting of
that new and highly persuasive, but clearly controversial, critical
approach to Cather as a writer.

Hermione Lee, as noted in chapter 7, pushes the connections between
biography and fiction harder perhaps than any other recent critic, but
her *Willa Cather: Double Lives* (1989) is a major contribution to analysis
and interpretation of Cather's novels as well. While accepting with some
equanimity the lesbian thesis advanced by O'Brien and others, Lee
assumes, if not quite a so-what attitude toward it, then at least a com-

monsense approach, warning readers and critics not to allow Cather's lesbianism to become the be-all and end-all as concerns either her life or her fiction.

The desire of radical feminists to see Cather's famous "thing not named" as a lesbian orientation that is both forbidden and the source of emotional strength in her fiction is, Lee believes, reductive, a gross over-simplification of the complexities of that fiction. On the other hand, she cites the lesbian connection whenever it suggests a good or clever point, as in her comparison of the Cather-Lewis relationship at 5 Bank Street in New York—Cather dominant, Lewis subservient—as being most appropriately comparable to the Gertrude Stein–Alice B. Toklas ménage at 27 rue de Fleurus in Paris. Her remarks on the Jaffrey, New Hampshire, gravesite are telling, Lewis being buried at Cather's *feet*. Lee concludes that at the heart of Cather's youthful enthusiasm for the stage is the "half-admitted" knowledge that "the theatre was a safe place for [Cather] to fall in love with great and beautiful women."[21] Lee seems to be the first major critic to come along who has the levelheaded capacity not to leap into the lesbianism fray either for or against, but simply to accept it and then move on to other topics of importance.

Lee's views on Cather's fiction are always insightful and sometimes aphoristic, as when she judges *The Troll Garden* to be "a negative performance, written out of a deep rage at the obstruction of the artist,"[22] or when she calls *The Song of the Lark* "a splendid source book for biographers."[23] About Cather's explanation for her 1920 trip to Europe—that it was motivated by a need to gather material for the French portions of *One of Ours*, then in the midst of composition—Lee offers a variant and surprisingly convincing opinion: Cather sailed for Europe less to investigate the aftermath of a terrible world war than to escape for a time an even more terrible America, whose postwar backlash and societal changes were depressing her.

Lee's discussion of *One of Ours* is, in fact, among her better analyses. Rather than approaching the novel as a study in Freudian psychology as Skaggs does (engrossingly), Lee perceives the book as an expression of Cather's innate romanticism as well as her profound failure to understand the true nature of modern warfare. She compares *One of Ours* with contemporary war books such as Cummings's *The Enormous Room* (1922) and Dos Passos's *One Man's Initiation: 1917* (1920) and *Three Soldiers* (1921), works that interpreted the war from an emotional stance of "profound disgust" akin to Ezra Pound's blast against a crumbling Western world in "Hugh Selwyn Mauberley" (1919):

> Died some, pro patria,
>
> non "dulce" non "et decor". . .
>
> Walked eye-deep in hell
>
> Believing in old men's lies, then unbelieving. . . .
>
> There died a myriad,
>
> And of the best, among them,
>
> For an old bitch gone in the teeth,
>
> For a botched civilization.[24]

Cather, on the other hand, says Lee, was still capable of taking inspiration from phrases such as "that rare privilege of dying well" and "it was the cause that made a man of him"[25]—precisely the type of language that writers such as Cummings and Dos Passos, and later Hemingway, considered not only dangerous but obscene as well.

The difference between Cather and her contemporaries would be clarified by events. In France, Claude Wheeler would find a Gothic church in which to sit and meditate on the happiness war had brought to him, whereas Dos Passos's Martin Howe would watch while his Gothic abbey was pounded to bits by explosive shells, bringing him to understand "that the war he is fighting means the destruction of the very civilization that he has fallen in love with."[26] Boiled down to essentials, for Lee Claude Wheeler is "a miserable, repressed Nebraskan boy who gets killed in a horrible war."[27] For her the novel is weighty with overtones of "sexual distress" in a hero who all too clearly is the mirror image of Cather herself. Claude's androgynous traits "are symptoms of the shaming sense that Cather herself had in her youth of being the wrong sex, or wrong for her sex."[28] As a youth, Claude is as feminine as he is masculine, an overmothered "unhappy virgin," but war transforms him into "a tall, muscular, red-headed pioneering soldier, protector of defenseless women and children, faithful companion, and brave warrior."[29] Lee is not edified.

Lee's treatment of *The Song of the Lark* is equally freighted with biographical overtones. It is, for her, by far Cather's "most personal and revealing novel,"[30] and had not Olive Fremstad fortuitously happened along to serve as a model for Thea, the book would have been Cather's autobiography, pure and simple, for "all the feelings are Cather's."[31] Thea shares every important ingredient of Cather's youthful "double life": the secret retreat of the attic room contrasted with the hurly-burly of everyday life in a large family, her adolescent hostility toward the ignorant philistines who populate her small town, and her passionate attachment to the western landscape, as well as her fierce need to achieve. Thea in Chicago is but a disguised version of Cather in Pittsburgh, and Thea, like Cather, is liberated into a true understanding of her vocation by way of a trip to the Southwest and her consequent discovery of cliff-dweller relics and their meaning.

This is a perceptive reading, one among the several merits that mark Lee's study as outstanding.

A nagging problem for scholars has been the placement of Cather in the modernist movement that dominates early twentieth-century literature in America. To make such a relationship is especially crucial in light of many modernist critics' rejection of any notion that Cather participates in the movement. They would instead classify her as an archconservative whose novels were overly simple, nonexperimental, and far from challenging intellectually. In such a view, Cather becomes irrelevant to modernism, she having rejected the present in favor of persistently focusing instead upon her nostalgia for a lost, heroic past.

This opinion is challenged directly by Jo Ann Middleton in her study *Willa Cather's Modernism* (1990). Middleton argues aggressively that Cather from her beginnings as a novelist was a dedicated experimentalist and that her theory expressed in "The Novel Démeublé" constitutes an individualistic form of minimalism. Middleton develops in particular Cather's use of the vacuole and the ambiguities these blanks or absences create, the way they urge the reader to participate in the writing of the story by filling in the blanks according to his own lights. And that is one mark of modernism generally agreed upon.

The ambiguity of the word *my* in the title *My Ántonia* is a case in point, one that has been discussed by any number of scholars. Middleton brings a new immediacy to the question. And she offers the word *lost* in the title *A Lost Lady* as a further instance. In what manner is Marian Forrester "lost," she would ask; and just whose "lost" lady is she—if she is anyone's? And why? Readers' individual repies to such queries will shape the "meaning" of a story and produce unique readings, says Middleton; and also, "The number of readings one can have is determined by the number of ways in which the reader can fill the vacuoles"[32] that characterize the structure of *A Lost Lady* and other Cather novels.

Another bit of evidence is offered—Cather's own words concerning the composition of *One of Ours*: "I have cut out all picture making because [Claude Wheeler] does not see pictures. It was hard to cease to do the thing that I do best, but we all have to pay the price for everything we accomplish."[33] The absences—the missing pictures—are for Middleton (although not for all critics) a vital clue to the characterization of Claude, for "what he does not see is essential to our understanding of him."[34] The Middleton thesis is of prime importance, of course, in approaching a novel such as *My Mortal Enemy*, which most would agree is Cather's principal example of the novel *démeublé* method put to practical use, so much so that it might be argued that its vacuoles outnumber and, indeed, "outweigh" the text itself.

Merrill Maguire Skaggs has served as mentor for any number of Cather scholars at Drew University Graduate School, and her comprehensive understanding of Cather is exhibited on every page of *After the World Broke in Two: The Later Novels of Willa Cather* (1990). The book takes its cue from Cather's famous and provocative declaration in *Not Under Forty* that the world she knew and loved broke in two "in 1922 or thereabouts" and that by lot or choice she belonged with those persons and attitudes that "slid back into yesterday's seven thousand years." While not assigning that breakup to any specific cause or event, Skaggs does agree that the novels of 1922 and after show considerable differences from those that had gone before. Their protagonists are more troubled, and their author, affected by "anger, disgust, and [a] sense of betrayal,"[35] is less optimistic in considering the ways of the world and the possibilities of happy outcomes. A mounting sense of despair haunts the writing.

Skaggs agrees with a good many of the current axioms regarding Cather: that, for instance, her books exist at an extrahigh level of biographical insight ("Willa Cather plays all the major roles in her own dramas"),[36] and that the novelist was among the most willing of American writers to attempt to invent new forms (she "repeatedly experimented in every volume, and . . . always brought off her experiments to artistic acclaim").[37] Skaggs is on firm ground here. But she has axioms of her own, some of them not quite so persuasive. One of these propositions says that Cather composed her post-1922 novels in pairs, as it were, the one being the converse of the other, so that, says Skaggs, Cather's novels "often stick together as opposite sides of a coin."[38] A nice figure, and one that works well as long as one is saying, for instance, that *The Professor's House*, with its "middle-aged male intellectual protagonist who feels intellectually dead," gives way to *My Mortal Enemy* and a "middle-aged female protagonist whose volcanic emotions are likely to erupt even when she is dying."[39] But to find oneself chained to such an axiom in cases considerably murkier can prove to be procrustean.

Something of the same holds true for Skaggs's emphasis upon the importance of names, a trap that can take one from the easy consensus regarding *Lucy Gayheart* to the merely speculative (that *Myra Driscoll* is intended to spur connections with "the possessive *my*"[40] as well as with *mine* and *drizzle* and *cold*) and from there to the rather mind-boggling suggestion that Sapphira Colbert's maiden name, *Dodderidge*, is somehow intended to bring the negatives *doddering* and *dodderer* to mind. These minor gaffes arrive as the end product of the belief that everything Cather allowed into her fiction was duly considered and deliberate, and that each word, phrase, and sentence means much more than it purports to mean. To place such interpretive weight upon names is a common failing among Cather scholars—though not among them alone, of course—and is a caution against investing too much critical capital in what seems a certain thing.

When Skaggs is successful—which is most of the time—she brings off brilliant effects. A case in point is her chapter on *One of Ours*, a compelling treatment of that novel as a study in Freudian psychology, and as fine a set of pages on Cather as I can recall reading. Skaggs takes her lead from a Cather conversation with Elizabeth Shepley Sergeant during which the great psychoanalyst's name came up. "Take this Viennese Freud: why was everybody reading him,"[41] Cather protested; didn't Tolstoy, didn't any other great novelist, have as full a command of psychology, and with no isms attached, as a fiction writer could ever need? Theory being one thing and practice another, Cather "systematically set out to psychoanalyze Claude Wheeler with Freudian categories [using] Freudian questions for the enterprise."[42]

Accordingly, *One of Ours* begins where it should, with Claude's childhood and his middle-of-three rank in birth order. The seductive favoritism shown him by his weak and ineffectual mother and the destructive ridicule, neglect, and overwork heaped upon him by his father make it inevitable that Claude will react with adoration of his mother, rage and hatred toward his father. Claude enters young manhood uncertain, frustrated, and despondent, filled with feelings of self-hate and what Skaggs calls a "meticulously elaborate psychological programming"[43] that leaves Claude physically normal and sound but psychologically a wreck, and deeply naive, particularly concerning women, unable to feel thoroughly comfortable with women other than motherly types. "Thus, Claude predictably picks the wrong bride"[44] for himself, a frigid version of his mother, and ends up frustrated sexually, starved intellectually, and out of place socially. His life on the Nebraska farm and in the hamlet of Frankfort becomes a living death.

When the opportunity comes for him to escape—by enlisting in the AEF to fight for another of his unrealistic ideals—Claude "leaps for it with eager ardor,"[45] becomes in a strange sense a war lover for whom the military uniform seems to change all aspects of his life from worse to better. Claude's death in France, ironically, seems not only proper but his true salvation, for not only does he die feeling that his life has achieved positive meaning, but his mother, who knows her son better than she usually will admit, understands that he could never have returned to his old life with any equanimity. In his death he finds his life. These pages on *One of Ours* are a masterly example of cogent reasoning backed up at every important point with the evidence that will convince the reader of their fundamental truth.

One of the most unusual and skillfully prepared books on Willa Cather ever to appear is *From Mesa Verde to "The Professor's House"* (1992), a study by David Harrell. With full-length biographies now abundant, as well as inclusive studies of Cather's fiction, Harrell's book undoubtedly points the way to the future in Cather studies: the close examination of key biographical and critical areas by scholar-writers well equipped for their task. That Harrell is one of those scholar-writers is revealed on every page of this investigation into Cather's links to the cliff-dwelling societies of the American Southwest, especially to those relics of the Anasazi that play a pivotal role in *The Song of the Lark* and stand at the center of *The Professor's House*. Cather invested relatively brief periods of time in visiting the ruins and studying about the cliff dwellers, but these extinct civilizations play a key role in her fiction; they provide Cather with an ancient, idealized, and lost civilization—but an *American* example—against which to juxtapose her contrasting disappointment in the wasteland aspects of modern times. Harrell places the entire topic under his literary microscope for scrutiny, with the objective of arriving at last at the truth so far as facts are concerned. The result is an ideal study in literary detective work.

When did Cather first gain substantial knowledge of the cliff dwellers? Aside from her 1912 trip with her brother Douglass to Walnut Canyon, Arizona, which served as the basis for Thea's similar experience three years later in *The Song of the Lark*, Harrell has been able to pinpoint the works of two important authors, "one of whom Cather mentions by name and the other whom she actually met."[46] Following her 1915 visit to Mesa Verde, Cather published a newspaper essay recounting her trip, a source unknown to most until it was unearthed and republished in 1984 by Bernice Slote and Susan Rosowski. That essay contains specific references to the first important Mesa Verde book, Gustaf Nordenskiold's *The Cliff Dwellers of the Mesa Verde* (1893), and establishes as fact Cather's having read it. Comparison of Nordenskiold with "Tom Outland's Story" indicates rather conclusively that Cather drew upon the book as a major source for her own fictional account. The other source was Clayton Wetherill, brother of the Colorado cowboy credited with discovery of the Mesa Verde Cliff Palace in 1888. Cather interviewed Clayton in Mancos, Colorado, in August 1915 and heard from his own lips the story of his brother Richard's discovery, on which important portions of "Tom Outland's Story" are based. (Since Harrell was able to determine that, by summer 1915, none of the five Wetherill brothers resided in Mancos, which had been their hometown, the precise methods by which he establishes that Clayton was in fact in temporary residence there and available to Cather provide a fascinating key to Harrell's status as a sleuth.)

On the actual visit to Mesa Verde, Cather was accompanied by her longtime companion Edith Lewis. That visit is given the closest scrutiny possible, in order to determine what Cather saw and heard, and when, and with or from whom. The itinerary of the visitors' railroad trip from Denver is reproduced in detail, as are their accommodations in Mancos, their method of reaching the mesa, and, in particular, their unique experience of being stranded in a mesa canyon overnight, an event that hit the news services and landed in the *New York Times*. Harrell is able to separate fact from fiction in the *Times* story and also to probe Lewis's version of the misadventure as recorded in her memoir *Willa Cather Living*. He demonstrates convincingly that Lewis's memory of events was unreliable. In departing momentarily from fact in order to indulge in speculation, Harrell suggests that it was perhaps during these several hours of enforced idleness, when Cather and Lewis were immobilized, in the darkness although safe, perched on a huge rock in the canyon, that Cather may have come to a decision in some fashion to use Mesa Verde in her fiction. What is known is that soon afterward she began to compose "The Blue Mesa," her first version of what would evolve into "Tom Outland's Story."

Because the literary significance of Cather's Mesa Verde experience rests upon her version of the discovery story used in *The Professor's House*, Harrell subjects that version to the same close examination. Cather claimed that in writing Tom Outland's account of discovering Cliff City she had followed very faithfully "the real story" as told to her by Clayton Wetherill. But this claim, put to the test, proves to be considerably less than true. Cather may well have believed that she was hewing close to her source, but Harrell establishes that she deviates from it at so many points that the fictional account becomes something quite different. The direction of change invariably tends in the direction of idealization, so that the Outland account emerges as "a new creation—its parts cleaner, simpler, and more ideal than those of the historical incident that inspired it."[47] In the fictional account, Blue Mesa is unexplored, remaining "a remote and mysterious challenge . . . yet to be claimed by someone [Tom Outland] worthy of it";[48] in reality, Mesa Verde prior to Wetherill had been rigorously explored by individuals and groups, many of its artifacts remained, and the ruins themselves had been "surveyed, mapped, sketched, photographed, and described."[49] Tom Outland is a sole discoverer; Richard Wetherill was accompanied by a brother-in-law. Outland first spies the ruins from a position below them; Wetherill was stationed on a canyon rim above them. Outland makes his discovery on the significant date of Christmas Eve; Wetherill found Cliff Palace on a more mundane date, 18 December. Outland does his utmost to preserve the secret of his find from the vulgarly curious; Wetherill at once drew a map for acquaintances showing just where Cliff Palace could be found, and he escorted tourists to it himself. Outland shies as clear as possible of money and museums; Wetherill sought out both, selling photographs as well as entire collections of relics. In fiction the Smithsonian turns a cold eye on Outland's attempt to preserve his findings for posterity; in real life the Smithsonian was considerably more receptive—and the approach was made not by Richard Wetherill but by his father, and not through a pilgrimage to Washington but through the U.S. mails. And there are many more divergences from the record, but if Cather's finished product is not the "real" story, concludes Harrell, it probably is a "better" story. Surely it provided Cather with an opportunity to insert into her novel, otherwise crammed with so much human concern for reputation, money, possession, and status, the contrasting portrait of an idealist with a genuine sense of history and a man uncontaminated by the modern urge for ego fulfillment.

The ultimate effect of Harrell's investigation is to reinforce Susan Rosowski's thesis by placing Cather solidly in the romantic tradition, where events and people can be simplified and idealized in order to strike the desired positive note. Harrell's is a valuable contribution to Cather studies, one with permanence, undoubtedly definitive. It is that rare thing, the volume that at once becomes indispensable to its subject. And it is written with such grace of style that it reads effortlessly, its unending parade of new revelations making it something of a page-turner, like a superior detective story, full of unearthed clues and testimony by hitherto-unknown witnesses, a revelation that throws the light of day into a dark corner.

The Future of Cather Studies

Cather scholars of the present generation have made great advances by concentrating on tasks both doable and asking to be done, but the terminus of Cather research is by no means in sight. Much remains, much that is already apparent, not to speculate on tasks that are unimaginable today but might (and undoubtedly will) become apparent with the passage of time and the emergence of new needs and new approaches to literary studies.

The first and most important order of business concerns the future of Cather's letters. Those now available for reading—perhaps as many as 2,000—have come to depositories scattered from coast to coast. The vagaries of depositors clearly motivated to secure their literary remains on familiar turf have produced odd results, frustrating to scholars. For instance, Cather's many letters to Zoe Akins reside in Pasadena, California, and despite the fine and lenient conditions under which these may be read at the Huntington Library, anyone interested in the words Cather wrote to another important contemporary, Dorothy Canfield Fisher, must plan on traveling 3,000 miles to the Guy Bailey Memorial Library in Burlington, Vermont. In the flat midsection of the nation, second home to Cather, one might review the novelist's letters to Irene Miner Weisz and others at Chicago's Newberry or scrutinize her messages to her early friends Carrie Miner Sherwood and Mariel Gere in Lincoln and Red Cloud, Nebraska. But the letters to another early friend, Louise Pound, are in Durham, North Carolina. Similarly, Cather's papers relating to her major publisher, Alfred A. Knopf, are in Austin, Texas; those relating to her first publisher, Houghton Mifflin, are in Cambridge, Massachusetts. Other letters rest in depositories equally distant by hundreds of miles from one another.

Two remedies suggest themselves. First is the bringing together *somehow* of all letters known to be extant into a single library. That goal represents an ideal, of course. One remedy might be for all present Cather depositories to issue photocopies of their holdings to all other depositories. That would have the practical advantage of making the Cather letters available to scholars at a dozen or more strategically placed research centers, which, as it happens, are readily accessible to most major geographic areas of the nation. Second and even more desirable is the actual publication of the Willa Cather letters in a complete and well-authenticated scholarly edition. The impossibility of such an edition coming about is by no means certain. The hurdles it must leap are not insuperable, for the wording of Cather's will does not constitute an absolute prohibition against publication; rather, it expresses a strong authorial preference. I believe that now, a half-century after Cather's departure from the scene, few doubt that her letters will ultimately come into print. It is time for some courageous university press to smash the ice jam, going through the courts if necessary.

At the same time, the search should continue for additional Cather letters, for it is certain that considerable numbers remain in private hands. The whereabouts of some are known, others not. Also, a determined search for letters *to* Cather should be undertaken. While we surmise that Cather destroyed her incoming mail before she died, less certain is that copies of her correspondents' letters no longer exist. Few if any of the writers appear to have made carbon copies of their personal mail, understandable in that the letters were invariably handwritten. But Cather may have returned letters to correspondents, as she seems to have requested these same writers to return hers, for destruction as it turned out. The glory of many collections of modern authors is that a scholar, without going beyond a single central institution, may examine *both* sides of a significant correspondence. The collections of E. E. Cummings (Harvard) and Theodore Dreiser (Pennsylvania) are prominent cases in point. To work the same advantage for Cather scholars seems eminently worth striving for.

Investigations into the private and professional dealings between Cather and her several major correspondents constitute another profitable direction for scholars. Cather's longtime relationships with contemporaries such as Akins and Fisher have as yet scarcely been touched. Of course, discovery of their letters to Cather would be of immeasurable help, but even lacking those, much can be done that would shed new light on Cather's life and works. The same holds true for Cather's dealings with her publishers, Knopf and Houghton Mifflin, as well as with her employer S. S. McClure, and the essential documents are accessible.

It will probably remain for a new and differently oriented generation to make the fullest application to Cather's fiction of new psychological theories, such as those of Jacques Lacan. But a good deal can already be done by scholars fortunate enough to be attuned to such new directions, which are proving to be profitable in connection with certain other American writers. And while no new "full dress" biography is anticipated for some time, substantial progress can be made by scholars who mine discrete bits of biography for the rich pockets of ore they contain. The work done by David Harrell in regard to Cather's 1915 trip to Mesa Verde and its significance to the novels serves as a model. The Nebraska background, so crucial to understanding Cather, has not been fully explored, and it needs to be investigated in depth by a native, one who comes to the task with a comprehensive grasp of both the facts and their significance. Too few present-day Cather scholars have led lives that would have prepared them adequately for such an undertaking.

The close examination of Cather's notes for writing, the various drafts of her fiction, her final-submission manuscripts, and her revisions (corrections made at both the galley- and page-proof stages) suggests another direction for critical pursuit that may never be possible unless major caches of Cather manuscript materials should come to light. What became of preliminary materials, so zealously preserved by some of Cather's contemporary writers, remains in her case something of a bewildering mystery, even though it is known that she sold some of her papers to collectors. Until and unless such papers are unearthed, the important analysis of Cather's working methods and revision practices will languish.

Finally, more needs to be done with the statements, often deliberately vague or ambiguous, that Cather was fond of spinning off when writing about her work or speaking about it impromptu. These include provocative statements such as her oft-quoted reference to the world breaking in two in 1922 "or thereabouts." Whatever that pronouncement was intended to mean (what break? whose world? what parameters on *thereabouts*?), prominent scholars today have taken irreconcilably differing tacks in interpreting it. Another such declaration is Cather's even more cryptic words to the effect that whatever exists on the page without being specifically named there constitutes the thing truly created. Such statements need to be explored, using every critical and psychological tool available.

As critical interest in Willa Cather edges its way toward the year 2000 and approaches the centenary observations of her major works, these seem to be some of the directions admiring readers need to understand more about, and they constitute directions scholars will undoubtedly take, to the enrichment of American letters.

Notes and References

Chapter One

1. James Woodress, *Willa Cather: A Literary Life* (Lincoln: University of Nebraska Press, 1987), xiv.
2. The role of the railroad in settling Nebraska is detailed in Richard Overton, *Burlington West* (Cambridge, Mass.: Harvard University Press, 1941), and also in *Burlington Route* (New York: Alfred A. Knopf, 1965).
3. Overton, *Burlington West*, 334, 352.
4. Materials covering the Cather family history are contained in a number of sources, including Mildred R. Bennett, *The World of Willa Cather* (New York: Dodd, Mead, 1951); Edith Lewis, *Willa Cather Living* (New York: Alfred A. Knopf, 1953), and, of course, Woodress, *A Literary Life*.
5. Willa Cather's account of her ride to the Catherton settlement is contained in a 1913 interview reprinted in Bernice Slote, *The Kingdom of Art* (Lincoln: University of Nebraska Press, 1966), 446–49.
6. Willa Cather, "Nebraska: The End of the First Cycle," *Nation* (5 September 1923): 237.
7. Slote, *Kingdom of Art*, 449.
8. The report of the Cather auction is as reprinted by the Willa Cather Pioneer Memorial from the *Red Cloud Commercial Advertiser*, 11 September 1884.
9. Bennett, *World of Cather*, 19–20.
10. Ibid., opposite p. 77, provides a photograph of the Cather-Miner troupe's *Beauty and the Beast* production of 1888.
11. Carrie Miner Sherwood, personal communication to author, 1966.
12. Bennett, *World of Cather*, 46–47.
13. Ibid., 75.
14. Ibid., 113.
15. E. K. Brown and Leon Edel, *Willa Cather: A Critical Biography* (New York: Alfred A. Knopf, 1953), 44.
16. Latrobe Carroll, "Willa Sibert Cather," *Bookman* 52 (May 1921): 214.
17. Mildred R. Bennett, ed., *Early Stories of Willa Cather* (New York: Dodd, Mead, 1957), 10.
18. Slote, *Kingdom of Art*, 13.
19. Ibid., 267–68.
20. Ibid., 17.
21. Ibid., 380–87.

Chapter Two

1. James Woodress, *A Literary Life*, 103–4.
2. Bennett, *Early Stories*, 110.
3. Elizabeth Moorhead, *These Too Were Here* (Pittsburgh: University of Pittsburgh Press, 1950), 47.
4. Willa Cather to Will Owen Jones, 29 September 1900, ALS, Alderman Library.
5. Moorhead, *These Too*, 50.
6. Ibid., 51.
7. Many features of Cather's life, such as her penchant during childhood and her university career for assuming masculine attire and nomenclature, as well as the virtual restriction to women of her intimate friendship and her excessive sense of privacy concerning her personal affairs, have led many first to speculate quietly and more recently to declare openly that Cather's orientation was lesbian. This topic is discussed further in chapter 7.
8. Willa Cather, *April Twilights* (New York: Alfred A. Knopf, 1933), 25.
9. Ibid., 35.
10. The epigraphs are most thoroughly examined by Slote, *Kingdom of Art*, 93–97.
11. Carroll, "Willa Sibert Cather," 214.
12. Willa Cather to Will Owen Jones, 7 May 1903, ALS, Alderman Library.
13. Ibid.
14. Ida M. Tarbell, *All in the Day's Work* (New York, 1939), 199; Lincoln Steffens, *The Autobiography of Lincoln Steffens* (New York, 1945), 361–63, 535.
15. Peter Lyon, *Success Story* (New York, 1963), 298.
16. Willa Cather, "148 Charles Street," in *Not Under Forty* (New York: Alfred A. Knopf, 1936), 52–75.
17. Ibid.
18. Ibid., 95.
19. Ibid., 88.
20. Ibid., 76.
21. The magazine serialization of McClure's life story is accompanied by a reference to Willa Cather's "invaluable assistance," but the book version states the case more emphatically: "I am indebted to the cooperation of Miss Willa Sibert Cather for the very existence of this book."
22. Annie Fields, ed., *Letters of Sarah Orne Jewett* (Boston: Houghton Mifflin, 1911), 249.
23. Ibid., 248.
24. Ibid., 247.

25.   Willa Cather, "My First Novels [There Were Two]," in *On Writing* (New York: Alfred A. Knopf, 1949), 91.

26.   Willa Cather, "The Bohemian Girl," *McClure's* (August 1912): 421.

27.   Mildred R. Bennett, personal communication to the author, 1966.

28.   Willa Cather to Elizabeth Sergeant, 20 April 1912, ALS, Alderman Library.

29.   Ibid.

30.   David Harrell, *From Mesa Verde to "The Professor's House"* (Albuquerque: University of New Mexico Press, 1992), 211.

31.   Edith Lewis, *Willa Cather Living* (New York, 1953), 99–102.

32.   Frederick Tabor Cooper, "O Pioneers!" *Bookman* (August 1913): 667.

33.   Frederick Tabor Cooper, "The Song of the Lark," *Bookman* (November 1915): 323.

34.   H. W. Boynton, "All Sorts," 495; Randolph Bourne, "Morals and Art from the West," *Dial* (14 December 1918): 557.

35.   "A Broken Epic," *Nation* (11 October 1922): 388; Robert Morss Lovett, "Americana," *New Republic* (11 October 1922): 178.

36.   See Jay B. Hubbell, *Who Are the Major American Writers?* (Durham, N.C.: Duke University Press, 1972), 165, 209, 219–21.

37.   Granville Hicks, "Bright Incidents," *Forum and Century* 86 (September 1931): vii; see also Hicks's "The Case against Willa Cather," in *Willa Cather and Her Critics*, ed. James Schroeter (Ithaca, N.Y.: Cornell University Press, 1967), 139–47.

Chapter Three

1.   Willa Cather, *Alexander's Bridge* (Boston: Houghton Mifflin, 1912), 11.

2.   Ibid., 84.

3.   Ibid., 146.

4.   Willa Cather, *O Pioneers!* (Boston: Houghton Mifflin, 1913), 104.

5.   Ibid., 98.

6.   Ibid., 88.

7.   Ibid., 124.

8.   Ibid., 102.

9.   Ibid.

10.   Ibid., 308.

11.   Willa Cather, *The Song of the Lark* (Boston: Houghton Mifflin, 1915), 76.

12.   Willa Cather, "Three American Singers," *McClure's* (December 1913): 48.

13.   Cather, *Lark*, 377.

14.   Ibid., 439.
15.   Ibid., 458.
16.   Ibid., 369.
17.   Ibid., 377.
18.   Ibid., 304, 306.
19.   Ibid., 571.
20.   Elizabeth Shepley Sergeant, *Willa Cather: A Memoir* (Lincoln: University of Nebraska Press, 1963), 139.
21.   Willa Cather, *My Ántonia* (Boston: Houghton Mifflin, 1918), 353.
22.   Ibid., 353.

Chapter Four

1.   Willa Cather, *One of Ours* (New York: Alfred A. Knopf, 1922), 103.
2.   Willa Cather, "Nebraska: The End of the First Cycle," *Nation* (5 September 1923): 238.
3.   Willa Cather, *Ours*, 419.
4.   Ibid., 458.
5.   Willa Cather, *A Lost Lady* (New York: Alfred A. Knopf, 1923), 9.
6.   Ibid., 110.
7.   Ibid., 111.
8.   Ibid., 114.
9.   Ibid., 170.
10.   Ibid.
11.   Ibid., 173.
12.   Willa Cather, *The Professor's House* (New York: Alfred A. Knopf, 1925), 32.
13.   Ibid., 90, 150.
14.   Ibid., 221.
15.   Ibid., 244.
16.   Ibid., 282.
17.   Willa Cather, *My Mortal Enemy* (New York: Alfred A. Knopf, 1926), 22.
18.   Ibid., 37.
19.   Ibid., 53.
20.   Ibid., 72.
21.   Ibid., 80.
22.   Ibid., 90–91.
23.   Ibid., 83.
24.   Ibid., 122.
25.   Willa Cather, *Death Comes for the Archbishop* (New York: Alfred A. Knopf, 1927), 7.
26.   Hubbell, *Who Are the Writers?* 164–65.

27. Ibid., 219–21.

28. T. K. Whipple, *Spokesmen* (New York: Appleton, 1928), 139.

Chapter Five

1. Willa Cather, *Shadows on the Rock* (New York: Alfred A. Knopf, 1931), 42.

2. Ibid.

3. Cited in Schroeter, *Cather and Critics*, 147.

4. "Home Grown Parnassian," *Time* (3 August 1931): 48.

5. Willa Cather, *Lucy Gayheart* (New York: Alfred A. Knopf, 1935), 23.

6. Ibid., 108–9.

7. Ibid., 3.

8. Ibid., 207.

9. Ibid.

10. Ibid., 77, 69, 156.

11. Ibid., 5.

12. Willa Cather, *Sapphira and the Slave Girl* (New York: Alfred A. Knopf, 1940), 137.

13. William H. Nolte, ed., *H. L. Mencken's "Smart Set" Criticism* (Ithaca, N.Y.: Cornell University Press, 1968), 263.

14. Cooper, "Lark," 152.

Chapter Six

1. Virginia Faulkner, ed., *Willa Cather's Collected Short Fiction*, rev. ed. (Lincoln: University of Nebraska Press, 1970), 495.

2. Ibid., 202.

3. Ibid.

4. Ibid., 242.

5. Ibid.

6. Ibid., 56.

7. Ibid., xxxiii.

8. Ibid., 34.

9. Ibid., 36.

10. Willa Cather, *Obscure Destinies*, (New York: Alfred A. Knopf, 1932), 77.

11. Ibid., 112–23.

12. Ibid., 107.

13. Ibid., 71.

Chapter Seven

1. William M. Curtin, ed., *The World and the Parish* (Lincoln: University of Nebraska Press, 1970), 2:881.

2. Thomas H. Johnson, ed., *The Letters of Emily Dickinson* (Cambridge, Mass.: Harvard University Press, 1958), 2:408.

3. *Willa Cather, A Biographical Sketch, Etc.* [a.k.a. "Knopf Pamphlet"] (New York: Alfred A. Knopf, 1928).

4. Ibid., 1.

5. Ibid., 2.

6. Elsie Goth, "Story by Willa Cather's Neighbors: As Told to Elsie Goth, *Nebraska Alumnus* 32 (April 1936): 6.

7. Phyllis C. Robinson, *Willa: The Life of Willa Cather* (New York: Doubleday, 1983), xi.

8. Ibid., 173.

9. Willa Cather to Elizabeth Shepley Sergeant, 26 April 1912, ALS, Newberry Library.

10. Ibid.

11. Woodress, *A Literary Life*, 294.

12. Ibid., 299.

13. Ibid., 141.

14. Sharon O'Brien, *Willa Cather: The Emerging Voice* (New York: Oxford University Press, 1987), 59.

15. Ibid., 53.

16. Hermione Lee, *Willa Cather: Double Lives* (New York: Pantheon, 1989), 17.

17. Ibid., 4.

18. Ibid., 11–12.

19. Ibid., 16.

20. Ibid., 81.

Chapter Eight

1. The data regarding Catherland and the WCPM derive from personal visits to Webster County and Red Cloud, 1965–93; from "We Have Reached the Twentieth Anniversary Milestone!" *WCPM Newsletter* (Spring 1975): 1–5; and from the one-page, triple-folded informational leaflet issued by the WCPM, c. 1975.

2. Susan J. Rosowski, *The Voyage Perilous: Willa Cather's Romanticism* (Lincoln: University of Nebraska Press, 1986), xiii.

3. Marilyn Arnold, *Willa Cather's Short Fiction* (Boston: G. K. Hall, 1984), xi.

4. Ibid., 88–89.

5. Ibid., 71.

6. Rosowski, *Voyage Perilous*, 248.

7. Ibid., 35.
8. Ibid., xi.
9. Ibid., xii.
10. Ibid., 62.
11. Ibid., 244.
12. Ibid., 63.
13. Ibid., 65.
14. Ibid., 68–69.
15. Ibid., 74.
16. Quoted from G. Richard Thompson in Rosowski, *Voyage Perilous*, 207.
17. Ibid., 222.
18. Ibid., 228.
19. John J. Murphy, *"My Ántonia": The Road Home* (New York: Twayne, 1989), 55.
20. Ibid., 105.
21. Lee, *Double Lives*, 53.
22. Ibid., 78.
23. Ibid., 120.
24. Quoted from Ezra Pound, "Hugh Selwyn Mauberley," in *The Norton Anthology of Modern Poetry*, ed. Richard Ellman and Robert O'Clair (New York: W. W. Norton, 1973), 346.
25. Lee, *Double Lives*, 169.
26. Ibid., 170.
27. Ibid., 179.
28. Ibid., 180.
29. Ibid.
30. Ibid., 120.
31. Ibid., 122.
32. Jo Ann Middleton, *Willa Cather's Modernism* (Rutherford, N.J.: Fairleigh Dickinson University Press, 1990), 61.
33. Ibid., 60; Cather quoted from a 1921 interview with Eva Mahoney.
34. Middleton, *Cather's Modernism*, 60.
35. Merrill Maguire Skaggs, *After the World Broke in Two: The Later Novels of Willa Cather* (Charlottesville: University Press of Virginia, 1990), 91.
36. Ibid., 113.
37. Ibid., 3.
38. Ibid., 27.
39. Ibid., 86.
40. Ibid., 94.
41. Ibid., 34.
42. Ibid.
43. Ibid., 36.
44. Ibid., 37.

45. Ibid.
46. Harrell, *Mesa Verde*, 13.
47. Ibid., 97.
48. Ibid., 98.
49. Ibid.

Selected Bibliography

PRIMARY SOURCES

Novels

Alexander's Bridge. Boston: Houghton Mifflin, 1912.
Death Comes for the Archbishop. New York: Alfred A. Knopf, 1927.
A Lost Lady. New York: Alfred A. Knopf, 1923.
Lucy Gayheart. New York: Alfred A. Knopf, 1935.
My Ántonia. Boston: Houghton Mifflin, 1918.
My Mortal Enemy. New York: Alfred A. Knopf, 1926.
One of Ours. New York: Alfred A. Knopf, 1922.
O Pioneers! Boston: Houghton Mifflin, 1913.
The Professor's House. New York: Alfred A. Knopf, 1925.
Sapphira and the Slave Girl. New York: Alfred A. Knopf, 1940.
Shadows on the Rock. New York: Alfred A. Knopf, 1931.
The Song of the Lark. Boston: Houghton Mifflin, 1915.

Short Story Collections

Obscure Destinies. New York: Alfred A. Knopf, 1932.
The Troll Garden. New York: McClure, Phillips, 1905.
Youth and the Bright Medusa. New York: Alfred A. Knopf, 1920.

Poems

April Twilights. Boston: R. G. Badger, 1903. Revised edition. New York: Alfred
   A. Knopf, 1923.

Essays

Not Under Forty. New York: Alfred A. Knopf, 1936.
Note: Willa Cather's novels, stories, poems, and essays were also published
(1937–41) by Houghton Mifflin in the 13-volume Library Edition.

Biography

The Life of Mary Baker G. Eddy and the History of Christian Science. New York:
   Doubleday, Page, 1909. Ostensibly by Georgine Milnine, but actually
   written by Cather.

My Autobiography. New York: Frederick A. Stokes, 1914. Ostensibly by S. S. McClure, but actually written by Cather.

Posthumous Publications

Collected Short Fiction, 1892–1912. Edited by Virginia Faulkner, with an introduction by Mildred R. Bennett. Lincoln: University of Nebraska Press, 1970. The most extensive and authoritative collection of Cather's early stories, reprinting works originally published during her college years, her career in Pittsburgh, and her tenure with *McClure's Magazine*.

Early Stories of Willa Cather. Selected and with commentary by Mildred R. Bennett. New York: Dodd, Mead, 1957. Reprints 19 stories written by Cather between 1892 and 1900 but uncollected by her.

Five Stories. New York: Alfred A. Knopf, 1956. Contains the first reprinting of "The Enchanted Bluff" (1909) as well as an essay by George S. Kates regarding Cather's unfinished Avignon story.

The Kingdom of Art. Edited by Bernice Slote. Lincoln: University of Nebraska Press, 1966. Cather's dramatic and literary criticism, 1893–96, supplemented by a valuable commentary by Slote.

The Old Beauty and Others. New York: Alfred A. Knopf, 1948. Stories.

Uncle Valentine and Other Stories. Edited by Bernice Slote. Lincoln: University of Nebraska Press, 1973. Completes the recovery of Cather's uncollected fiction from 1915 through 1929. Notable for its comparison of the texts of "Coming, Eden Bower!" and "Coming, Aphrodite!"

Willa Cather in Europe. New York: Alfred A. Knopf, 1956. Reprinting of Cather's journalistic reports from Europe, 1902, with an introduction by George N. Kates.

Willa Cather in Person. Edited by L. Brent Bohlke. Lincoln: University of Nebraska Press, 1986. Interviews and speeches by Cather plus the handful of letters published during her lifetime.

Willa Cather on Writing. New York: Alfred A. Knopf, 1949. Essays.

The World and the Parish. Edited by William M. Curtin. 2 vols. Lincoln: University of Nebraska Press, 1970. Indispensable collection of Cather's journalism 1893–1902.

Writings from Willa Cather's Campus Years. Edited by James R. Shively. Lincoln: University of Nebraska Press, 1950. The first, incomplete reprinting of dramatic criticism and fiction written during 1892–95, a selection accompanied by comments about Cather made by her former college classmates.

SECONDARY SOURCES

Bibliography

Arnold, Marilyn. *Willa Cather: A Reference Guide*. Boston: G. K. Hall, 1986. An extremely valuable compilation of writings about Cather from 1895 through 1984, annotated by Arnold.

Crane, Joan. *Willa Cather: A Bibliography*. Lincoln: University of Nebraska Press, 1982. A definitive listing, with full bibliographic description, of all of Cather's writings.

Biography (Books and Parts of Books)

Ambrose, Jamie. *Willa Cather: Writing at the Frontier*. Oxford: Berg Publishers, 1988. A reasonable account of Cather's life but incomplete and sometimes inaccurate in its details, with notes and a bibliography that are of little use for scholarly purposes.

Bennett, Mildred R. *The World of Willa Cather*. New York: Dodd, Mead, 1951. Reprint, with notes and index, Lincoln: University of Nebraska Press, 1961. A close examination, in situ, of Cather's Nebraska background, prepared with the cooperation of many who knew Cather and the models for places or persons in her fiction.

Brown, E. K., and Leon Edel. *Willa Cather: A Critical Biography*. New York: Alfred A. Knopf, 1953. The most substantial biographical record prior to Woodress (1987) and still a reliable text.

Brown, Marian Marsh, and Ruth Crone. *Only One Point of the Compass; Willa Cather in the Northeast*. Danbury, Conn.: Archer Editions Press, 1980. Deals chiefly with Cather's summer residence on Grand Manan Island. Sadly, undocumented.

Butcher, Fanny. *Many Lives—One Love*. New York: Harper & Row, 1972. A chapter is devoted to reminiscences of Cather, whom Butcher knew from 1912 to 1947.

Byrne, Kathleen D., and Richard C. Snyder. *Chrysalis: Willa Cather in Pittsburgh*. Pittsburgh: Historical Society of Western Pennsylvania, 1980. Augments Moorhead, pulling together what is known about Cather and her friends in Pittsburgh.

Lewis, Edith. *Willa Cather Living*. New York: Alfred A. Knopf, 1953. Informal, incomplete, and undoubtedly biased, but important because written by the companion who shared living quarters with Cather for 40 years.

Moorhead, Elizabeth. *These Too Were Here*. Pittsburgh: University of Pittsburgh Press, 1950. A reminiscence of Louise Homer and Willa Cather, slight but important on Cather's Pittsburgh life because written by one who knew her there and then.

O'Brien, Sharon. *Willa Cather: The Emerging Voice*. New York: Oxford University Press, 1987. An exciting revisionary study, examined in detail in chapter 7.

Robinson, Phyllis C. *Willa: The Life of Willa Cather*. Garden City, N.Y.: Doubleday, 1983. A readable biography and the first to apply the lesbian label to Cather, but not highly regarded by scholars.

Sergeant, Elizabeth Shepley. *Willa Cather: A Memoir*. Lincoln: University of Nebraska Press, 1963. Reminiscences by a lifelong friend, with an emphasis upon the years 1910–31. An indispensable source.

Slote, Bernice. *Willa Cather: A Pictorial Memoir*. Photographs by Lucia Woods and others. Lincoln: University of Nebraska Press, 1974. A comprehensive volume of Cather photographs, including many that illustrate her locales and characters.

Woodress, James. *Willa Cather: Her Life and Art*. New York: Pegasus, 1970. Superseded by Woodress's second biography, but a valuable text in its own right.

———. *Willa Cather: A Literary Life*. Lincoln: University of Nebraska Press, 1987. The definitive biography, reviewed in chapter 7.

Criticism (Collections)

Bennett, Mildred R., and Susan J. Rosowski, eds. *Great Plains Quarterly* 4 (Fall 1984): 211–27. Important essays by Arnold, Bohlke, Miller, Murphy, Pers, Rosowski, and Woods.

Murphy, John J., ed. *Critical Essays on Willa Cather*. Boston: G. K. Hall, 1984. Thirty-five essays and reviews by E. and L. Bloom, Bourne, Brande, Canby, Comeau, Cooper, Cooperman, Cross, Dronenberger, Edel, Eichorn, Fisher, Forman, Gelfant, George, Giannone, Helmick, Keeler, Mencken, Murphy, Nichols, Poore, Porter, Randall, Slote, Stouck, Stuart, Welty, and Woodress.

———, ed. *Five Essays on Willa Cather: The Merrimack Symposium*. North Andover, Mass.: Merrimack College, 1974. Important essays by L. Bloom, Giannone, Murphy, Randall, and Slote.

———, ed. *Great Plains Quarterly* 2 (Fall 1982): 193–248. Important Cather essays by Baker, Bennett, Murphy, Rosowski, Slote, Stouck, Woodress.

———, ed. *Literature and Belief* 8 (1988): 1–130. The religious element in Cather's writing, a topic all too seldom addressed, serves as focus for valuable essays by Arnold, Baker, Bennett, Blanch, Larsen, Murphy, Pulsipher, Rosowski, Skaggs, Stouck, and Tanner.

O'Connor, Margaret Anne, ed. *Women's Studies* 2 (December 1984): 219–371. Important essays by Arnold, Briggs, Cousineau, Griffiths, Grumbach, Hamner, Morrow, O'Connor, Pannill, Rich, Rosowski, and Ryerson.

Rosowski, Susan J., ed. *Cather Studies 1*. Lincoln: University of Nebraska Press, 1990. Premiere volume of an important series. Cather essays by Briggs,

Fisher-Wirth, Harrell, Harris, Madigan, Murphy, Romines, Rosowski, Schwind, Stouck, Swift, and Woodress.

————, ed. *Cather Studies 2*. Lincoln: University of Nebraska Press, 1993. Important Cather essays by Chown, Fisher-Wirth, Flanigan, Miller, Schubnell, Schwind, Skaggs, Wasserman, and Woodress.

Schroeter, James, ed. *Willa Cather and Her Critics*. Ithaca: Cornell University Press, 1967. Important reviews and essays by Bloom, Bogan, Brown, Commanger, Daiches, Edel, Geismar, Hicks, Jones, Kazin, Krutch, Lewis, Mencken, Moorhead, Randall, Schloss, Schroeter, Sergeant, Slote, Van Doren, West, Whipple, Wilson, and Zabel.

Stuckey, William J., ed. *Modern Fiction Studies* 36 (Spring 1990): 3–129. Important Cather essays by Dysek, Gelfant, Haller, Harris, Irving, Peck, Strychacz, Summers, and Wasserman.

Criticism (Books and Parts of Books)

Adams, J. Donald. *The Shape of Books to Come*. New York: Viking Press, 1944. Cather approached, toward the end of her life, as an artist of high seriousness, one who places more stress on themes than subject matter. An eloquent defense against Marxist derogation.

Arnold, Marilyn. *Willa Cather's Short Fiction*. Athens: Ohio University Press, 1984. An excellent study, reviewed in chapter 8.

Auchincloss, Louis. *Pioneers and Caretakers*. Minneapolis: University of Minnesota Press, 1965. An astute assessment that places *My Mortal Enemy* among Cather's finest work and considers Cather within a context of other twentieth-century American women authors.

Berkove, Lawrence I. "*A Lost Lady*: The Portrait of a Survivor." In *The Mildred Bennett Festschrift: In Observance of Her Eightieth Birthday*, edited by Debbie A. Hanson, 55–68. Lewiston, N.Y.: Edwin Mellen Press, 1991. A close examination of the life of Marian Forrester, to emphasize her drive for survival and draw parallels between her and Cather.

Bloom, Edward A., and Lillian D. Bloom. *Willa Cather's Gift of Sympathy*. Carbondale: Southern Illinois University Press, 1962. A perceptive analysis of Cather's themes and techniques, valuable for its chapter on the composition of *Death Comes for the Archbishop*.

Boynton, Percy H. *Some Contemporary Americans*. Chicago: University of Chicago Press, 1924. Perceptive chapter on Cather's development as an artist that finds her, in 1924, somewhat off course with *One of Ours* and *A Lost Lady*.

Callander, Marilyn Berg. *Willa Cather and the Fairy Tale*. Ann Arbor, Mich.: UMI Research Press, 1989. An interesting but overly specialized study whose message is that fairy tales often were uppermost in Cather's mind as she wrote her fiction.

Connolly, Francis X. "Willa Cather: Memory as Muse." In *Fifty Years of the American Novel*, edited by Harold C. Gardiner, S.J., 69–87. New York:

Charles Scribner's Sons, 1951. *My Ántonia*, *The Professor's House*, and *Death Comes for the Archbishop* are considered to be crucial in terms of Cather's "passion for order" and the limitations that passion imposed upon her fiction.

Cooperman, Stanley. "Willa Cather and the Bright Face of Death." In *World War One and the American Novel*, 129–37. Baltimore: Johns Hopkins University Press, 1967. An illuminating consideration of *One of Ours* regarded in the context of other American war novels.

Fryer, Judith. *Felicitious Space: The Imaginative Structures of Edith Wharton and Willa Cather*. Chapel Hill: University of North Carolina Press, 1986. Focuses on the connection between space and the female imagination, with a confusing organizational pattern that makes it difficult for the reader who wishes to study only the Cather portions.

Geismar, Maxwell. *The Last of the Provincials*. Boston: Houghton Mifflin, 1947. General appraisal of Cather in her times, centering on the "cultural wound" inflicted by the dominance of an emerging industrialism whose sad implications Cather portrayed only indirectly. Considers *Lucy Gayheart* to be one of Cather's most convincing novels.

Gelfant, Blanche. "Movement and Melody: The Disembodiment of Lucy Gayheart." *Women Writing on America: Voices in Collage*. Hanover, N.H.: University Press of New England, 1984. Argues that *Lucy Gayheart* warrants a reconsideration based on the thesis that Cather deliberately took a gamble by selecting as a pre-text the conventional love story, which heretofore she had avoided, with the intention of transforming it into something quite different.

Gerber, Philip. *Willa Cather*. Boston: Twayne, 1975. A general biographical/critical study that Woodress calls "a good place for a beginner to approach Cather." Extensively reorganized and revised for the present edition (1995).

Giannone, Richard. *Music in Willa Cather's Fiction*. Lincoln: University of Nebraska Press, 1966. Specialized but persuasive study of the centrality of music in Cather's fiction and its influence upon theme, characterization, and form.

Harrell, David. *From Mesa Verde to "The Professor's House."* Albuquerque: University of New Mexico Press, 1992. A superior study, reviewed at length in chapter 8.

Hartwick, Harry. *The Foreground of American Fiction*. New York: American Book, 1934. An early estimate of Cather's position in literary history, emphasizing her differences from the naturalists.

Hoffman, Frederick J. *The Twenties*. Revised edition. New York: Free Press, 1962. Presents *The Professor's House* as being a key novel in depicting the clash between the modern and the traditional.

Jones, Howard Mumford. *The Bright Medusa*. Urbana: University of Illinois Press, 1952. Denies that Cather withdrew from life; she merely lived it on another plane. Praising of Cather's sense of life's dignity.

Kazin, Alfred. *On Native Grounds*. New York: Reynall & Hitchcock, 1942. Sees Cather as an elegist for a lost world of tradition that she considers to have been grander than its modern substitute.

Levy, Helen Fiddyment. "Damning the Stream: Willa Cather." In *Fiction of the Home Place*, 64–96. Jackson: University Press of Mississippi, 1992. Explores the significant links between the daily work of women and their creativity, citing selected Cather novels and stories.

McFarland, Dorothy Tuck. *Willa Cather*. New York: Frederick Ungar, 1972. A brief, interesting treatment by a biographer-critic who suggests that everything Cather wrote ultimately adds to a metaphor of the conflict within Cather herself: is the world to be seen as scientific reason shows it to be, or as we wish it might be?

Mencken, H. L. "Willa Cather." In *The Borzoi, 1920*, 28–31. New York: Alfred A. Knopf, 1920. Important for its timing and for its summary of the opinions of an early Cather booster, who saw her early on as a mature and even major writer.

Middleton, Jo Ann. *Willa Cather's Modernism*. Rutherford, N.J.: Fairleigh Dickinson University Press, 1990. An important work, reviewed at length in chapter 8.

Moers, Ellen. *Literary Women*. New York: Oxford University Press, 1985. Considers Cather within a historical spread of women who wrote fiction and poetry. Sees *A Lost Lady* as "an Electra story" and *The Song of the Lark* as containing "the most thoroughly elaborated female landscape in literature."

Murphy, John J. *"My Ántonia": The Road Home*. New York: Twayne, 1989. A thorough examination, reviewed in chapter 8.

Nelson, Robert J. *Willa Cather and France*. Urbana: University of Illinois Press, 1988. Concentrates on Cather's Francophilia as it shows up in her fiction from her first story, "Peter," to her final novel, *Sapphira and the Slave Girl*.

Randall, John H. III. *The Landscape and the Looking Glass*. Boston: Houghton Mifflin, 1960. Penetrating analysis of Cather's novels, centering on her search for value, balancing her strengths and weaknesses as a writer. A relatively early, and major, study.

Rapin, René. *Willa Cather*. Robert M. McBride, 1930. The first critical volume devoted to Cather, noted for its independent judgments of *One of Ours* as belonging among Cather's best work, *A Lost Lady* among her minor efforts.

Rosowski, Susan J. *The Voyage Perilous: Willa Cather's Romanticism*. Lincoln: University of Nebraska Press, 1986. A superior work, reviewed at length in chapter 8.

————, ed. *Approaches to Teaching Cather's "My Ántonia."* New York: Modern Language Association of America, 1989. A collaborative effort, teaching materials on all aspects of the novel; contributions by Bair, Bradley, Cherny, Comeau, Evans, Ferguson, Gelfant, Gerber, Goodman, Love, McNall, Mierendorf, Murphy, O'Brien, Olson, Peterman, Quirk, Rosowski, Schwind, Stouck, Tatum, Thacher, Wasserman, and Woodress.

Ryder, Mary. *Willa Cather and Classical Myth: The Search for a New Parnassus.* Lewiston, N.Y.: Edwin Mellen Press, 1990. Exhaustive exploration of the classical myths known to Cather and utilized in her writing.

Sergeant, Elizabeth Shepley. *Fire under the Andes.* New York: Alfred A. Knopf, 1927. Sergeant's essay on Cather traces the development of her reputation and links her works closely with her biography.

Sherman, Stuart. *Critical Woodcuts.* New York: Charles Scribner's Sons, 1926. Chapter on Cather sees the vital center of her novels being the individual's efforts to live up to his potentialities.

Slote, Bernice, and Virginia Faulkner, eds. *The Art of Willa Cather.* Lincoln: University of Nebraska Press, 1974. Proceedings of the international seminar held in observation of the Cather centennial.

Thurin, Erik Ingvar. *The Humanization of Willa Cather: Classicism in an American Classic.* Lund, Sweden: Lund University Press, 1990. A Swedish scholar examines Cather's use of the classics in her novels, stories, poetry, journalism, and letters.

Woodress, James. "Willa Cather." In *Sixteen Modern American Authors.* Vol. 2, *A Survey of Research and Criticism since 1972,* edited by Jackson R. Bryer, 42–72. Durham, N.C.: Duke University Press, 1990. The latest update of this regularly revised review of scholarly activity concerning writers from Sherwood Anderson to Thomas Wolfe. The best and most complete place to begin when a survey is wanted of what has been written, who wrote it, and how it stands up relative to other scholarship. An indispensable source.

Criticism (Periodicals)

Note: Essays already listed in the "Criticism (Collections)" section are not listed separately here.

Ammons, Elizabeth. "The Engineer as Cultural Hero and Willa Cather's First Novel, *Alexander's Bridge." American Quarterly* (Winter 1986): 746–60. A fascinating essay comparing *Alexander's Bridge* with other cultural works concerned with the rise of the mystique of engineers that raised these wizards of the material to the status of national icon during the early years of the twentieth century.

Arnold, Marilyn. "The Other Side of Willa Cather." *Nebraska History* 68 (Summer 1987): 74–82. Centers on Cather's physical presence and personality, primarily by way of an extensive gathering of descriptive remarks (often conflicting) by "casual observers" who met Cather only briefly but recorded their impressions.

————. "Willa Cather's `Artistic Radicalism.'" *CEA Critic* 51 (Summer 1989): 2–10. Reviews the literature responsible for establishing the image of Cather as a conforming traditionalist, refuting it with Cather's own statements regarding her commitment to experimentation.

Baum, Bernard. "Willa Cather's Waste Land." *South Atlantic Quarterly* 48 (October 1949): 589–601. Persuasive essay linking Cather with the widespread "waste land" spirit of the 1920s, allying her thematically with Eliot, Fitzgerald, Ransom, MacLeish, Tate, and others.

Bennett, Mildred R. "How Willa Cather Chose Her Names." *Names* 10 (March 1962): 29–37. An interesting example of Bennett's investigations into Nebraska source materials for Cather's fiction.

Faber, Rebecca J. "Some of His: Cather's Use of Dr. Sweeney's Diary in *One of Ours*." *WCPM Newsletter* (Spring 1993): 5–9. Explains in fascinating detail the manner and degree to which Cather used the wartime diary of Dr. Frederick Sweeney as a source for part 4 of *One of Ours*, "The Voyage of the Anchises."

Fadiman, Clifton. "Willa Cather: The Past Recaptured." *Nation* (7 December 1932): 563–65. A rather typical 1930s assessment in which Cather's "hypertrophied" sense of the past is seen as a threat to her position as a major artist. Important as a key to the period.

Fisher-Wirth, Ann W. "Reading Marian Forrester." *Legacy: A Journal of Women Writers* 9 (1992): 35–48. A psychoanalytic study of the heroine of *A Lost Lady*, showing Neil Herbert's fascination with and fear of Marian's sexuality.

Footman, Robert H. "The Genius of Willa Cather." *American Literature* 10 (May 1938): 123–41. Uses Cather's limitations (here meaning her economic, religious, and aesthetic motivations) as a means of defining her genius; an important early appraisal in refutation of the usual 1930s judgment on Cather.

Gerber, Philip. "Willa Cather and the Big Red Rock." *College English* 19 (January 1958): 152–57. Examines the thematic implications of the rock symbol in Cather's stories and novels.

Hinz, John. "*A Lost Lady* and *The Professor's House*." *Virginia Quarterly Review* 29 (Winter 1953): 70–85. An original and early analysis of *The Professor's House* in the context of its times and of Cather's life. Links the novel with Cather's early story "The Professor's Commencement" (1902).

Jones, Howard Mumford. "The Novels of Willa Cather." *Saturday Review of Literature* (6 August 1938): 3–4, 16. Cather's contribution assessed upon publication of her Library Edition, with a defense of Cather's lack of interest in people as creatures of economics.

Kronenberger, Louis. "Willa Cather." *Bookman* 74 (October 1931): 134–40.
Appraises Cather as the most human and solid of contemporary novelists,
but sees her moving in the wrong direction with *Shadows on the Rock*.

Martin, Terence. "The Drama of Memory in *My Ántonia*." *PMLA* 84 (March
1969): 304–11. Jim Burden, as narrator of the novel, reveals his own
story and also the reasons why Ántonia epitomizes human values for him.

Morris, Lloyd. "Willa Cather." *North American Review* 219 (April 1924):
641–52. An important early assessment of Cather, her strengths and
weaknesses, seeing her as celebrant of a lost tradition having no adequate
modern parallel.

Morrow, Nancy. "Willa Cather's *A Lost Lady* and the Nineteenth-Century
Novel of Adultery." *Women's Studies* 11 (December 1984): 287–303.
Disagrees with those who see a valid comparison between *A Lost Lady*
and *Madame Bovary*, for Cather's story is unconcerned with traditional
moral issues and the impact of adultery on family stability.

Murphy, John J. "Cooper, Cather, and the Downward Path to Progress." *Prairie
Schooner* 55 (Spring/Summer 1981): 168–84. Cooper's frontier and
Cather's frontier are compared, demonstrating that in both instances the
idealism of early settlers is overwhelmed by the destructive materialism of
the lesser generation that succeeds them.

———. "Willa Cather and Hawthorne." *Renascence* 27 (Spring 1975): 161–75.
Explores the similarities between selected works by Cather and
Hawthorne, a comparison of *A Lost Lady* with "Rappaccini's Daughter"
being a representative example.

Rosowski, Susan J. "Willa Cather's *A Lost Lady*: The Paradoxes of Change."
Novel 11 (Fall 1977): 31–62. Contradicts the view that *A Lost Lady* is
merely "an elegy for the pioneer past" and limited to a specific time and
place, replacing that view by stressing instead the universal theme of
change and the difficulty of adapting the best into the inevitable new.
Marian Forrester is seen as a life force with a transforming impact on
those around her.

———, and Bernice Slote. "Willa Cather's 1916 Mesa Verde Essay: The
Genesis of *The Professor's House*." *Prairie Schooner* 58 (Winter 1984):
81–92. Presents and reprints an extremely important discovery in source
materials in which Cather tells in her own words the story of her Mesa
Verde adventure, explaining also what and who she has been reading and
speaking to on the topic of the cliff dwellers.

Schwind, Jean. "The Benda Illustrations to *My Ántonia*: Cather's 'Silent'
Supplement to Jim Burden's Narrative." *PMLA* 100 (January 1985):
51–67. An unusual essay, reproducing the Benda illustrations and
explaining their use as a realistic counterpart to the romanticism of Jim
Burden's memoir.

———. "The 'Beautiful' War in *One of Ours*." *Modern Fiction Studies* 30 (Spring
1984): 53–71. Disagrees with critics who see Cather's World War I as an

authorial idealization, creating a field of action whereon Claude Wheeler "finds himself." Instead, the idealization is Claude's. He misses the bitter irony of his death, and too many readers and critics seem to miss the irony of it also.

Skaggs, Merrill Maguire. "*Death Comes for the Archbishop*: Cather's Mystery and Manner." *American Literature* 57 (October 1985): 395–406. Argues that after attempting only semisuccessfully to blend the themes of art and religion in *My Mortal Enemy*, Cather in her next and major effort, *Death Comes for the Archbishop*, achieved her aim.

———. "A Glance into *The Professor's House*: Inward and Outward Bound." *Renascence* 39 (Spring 1987): 422–28. Development of Augusta and Tom Outland are used to aid in clarifying Godfrey St. Peter's crisis and his eventual handling of it by letting go with the heart.

———. "Poe's Shadow on *Alexander's Bridge*." *Mississippi Quarterly* 35 (Fall 1982): 365–74. When Cather came to perceive the many obvious parallels between her first novel and "The Fall of the House of Usher," says Skaggs, she was influenced to reject *Alexander's Bridge*.

———. "Willa Cather's Experimental Southern Novel." *Mississippi Quarterly* 35 (Winter 1981): 3–14. Argues that Cather's return to her Virginia roots in *Sapphira and the Slave Girl* was motivated by a wish to challenge literary notions concerning antebellum southern life and the stereotype of the "lady," as well as to experiment with a new form of narrative.

Wasserman, Loretta. "*Sapphira and the Slave Girl*: Willa Cather vs. Margaret Mitchell." *WCPM Newsletter* (Spring 1994): 1, 3, 5, 7, 9, 11, 13, 15. A timely comparison of *Sapphira and the Slave Girl* with *Gone with the Wind*, especially as it concerns the portrayal of black characters, attitudes expressed toward them, and language employed anent them.

Winsten, Archer. "A Defense of Willa Cather." *Bookman* 74 (March 1932): 634–40. A lively defense of Cather against the Marxist critics' attacks just then getting under way.

Yongue, Patricia Lee. "Willa Cather's Aristocrats." *Southern Humanities Review* 14 (Winter 1980): 43–56, and (Spring 1980): 111–25. A two-part revisionary portrait based on Slote's opinion that Cather longed to be "a lady" such as her mother. Yongue examines Cather's worldliness, her inordinate respect for people of "wealth and aesthetic sensibility" (such as Stephen Tennant). Cather's admiration for the rugged pioneer contrasts with her distaste for the "vulgarity" of earning one's daily living. Characters such as Alexandra Bergson, Myra Henshawe, and Marian Forrester become important examples of the aristocratic ideal.

———. "Edith Lewis Living." *WCPM Newsletter* (Fall 1987): 12–15. Examines the crucial role played by Lewis in controlling the image of Cather that was to be presented in Brown-Edel and in her own memoir.

Index

The Author

Philip Gerber, professor of English at the State University of New York, is the author of *Robert Frost, Willa Cather* (1975), and *Theodore Dreiser* in Twayne's United States Authors Series. He has published *Plots and Characters in the Fiction of Theodore Dreiser* as well as a number of composition texts. His most recent book is *Bachelor Bess: The Homesteading Letters of Elizabeth Corey, 1909–1919*. Professor Gerber has served as president of the New York State branches of the American Studies Association and the College English Association, and he is a member of the editorial board for the University of Pennsylvania edition of Theodore Dreiser. In 1989 he was president of the Robert Frost Society and in 1990 was the recipient of the MidAmerica Award for distinguished contributions to the study of midwestern literature.

The Editor

Joseph M. Flora earned his B.A. (1956), M.A. (1957), and Ph.D. (1962) in English at the University of Michigan. In 1962 he joined the faculty of the University of North Carolina, where he is now professor of English. His study *Hemingway's Nick Adams* (1984) won the Mayflower Award. He is also author of *Vardis Fisher* (1962), *William Ernest Henley* (1970), *Frederick Manfred* (1974), and *Ernest Hemingway: A Study of the Short Fiction* (1989). He is editor of *The English Short Story* (1985) and coeditor of *Southern Writers: A Biographical Dictionary* (1970), *Fifty Southern Writers before 1900* (1987), *Fifty Southern Writers after 1900* (1987), *Contemporary Fiction Writers of the South* (1993), and *Contemporary Poets, Dramatists, Essayists, and Novelists of the South* (1994). He serves on the editorial boards of *Studies in Short Fiction* and *Southern Literary Journal*.